NEW DIRECTIONS FOR HIGHER EDUCATION

Martin Kramer, *University of California, Berkeley*
EDITOR-IN-CHIEF

The Campus and Environmental Responsibility

David J. Eagan
University of Wisconsin, Madison

David W. Orr
Oberlin College

EDITORS

Number 77, Spring 1992

JOSSEY-BASS PUBLISHERS
San Francisco

THE CAMPUS AND ENVIRONMENTAL RESPONSIBILITY
David J. Eagan, David W. Orr (eds.)
New Directions for Higher Education, no. 77
Volume XX, number 1
Martin Kramer, Editor-in-Chief

Microfilm copies of issues and articles are available in 16mm and 35mm,
as well as microfiche in 105mm, through University Microfilms Inc., 300
North Zeeb Road, Ann Arbor, Michigan 48106.

LC 85-644752   ISSN 0271-0560   ISBN 1-55542-753-7

NEW DIRECTIONS FOR HIGHER EDUCATION is part of The Jossey-Bass
Higher and Adult Education Series and is published quarterly by Jossey-
Bass Inc., Publishers, 350 Sansome Street, San Francisco, California 94104-
1310 (publication number USPS 990-880). Second-class postage paid at
San Francisco, California, and at additional mailing offices. POSTMASTER:
Send address changes to New Directions for Higher Education, Jossey-
Bass Inc., Publishers, 350 Sansome Street, San Francisco, California 94104-
1310.

SUBSCRIPTIONS for 1992 cost $45.00 for individuals and $60.00 for institutions, agencies, and libraries.

EDITORIAL CORRESPONDENCE should be sent to the Editor-in-Chief,
Martin Kramer, 2807 Shasta Road, Berkeley, California 94708.

Cover photograph and random dot by Richard Blair/Color & Light © 1990.

 The paper used in this book is acid-free and meets California
requirements for recycled paper (50 percent recycled waste including 10 percent postconsumer waste), which are the strictest guidelines for recycled paper currently in use in the United States.

Manufactured in the United States of America.

CONTENTS

EDITORS' NOTES

In a commencement address a few years ago, poet, philosopher, and farmer Wendell Berry raised a simple but nearly impossible challenge. "Find work, if you can," he said, "that does no damage" to the world or to its future. Had he addressed the same students four years before at their high school graduations, saying, "Find a *college,* if you can, that does no damage," where would they have gone? How many institutions even now have bothered to analyze their resource flows of energy, water, materials, food, and waste? How many have attempted to implement environmental standards for landscaping or new construction? How many have attempted to minimize the damage that they do to the world that their graduates will inherit? How many of the proudest of our colleges and universities educate their graduates even to understand the problem? The answers are clearly "not many," perhaps not even "a few." But things are changing, and some of those changes are described in this volume, *The Campus and Environmental Responsibility.*

The decade of the 1990s represents a confluence of opportunities and challenges. Seldom in history has the world of education been so stressed by high expectations, political demands, and financial constraints. Yet, seldom, if ever, have the opportunities for constructive change been greater. These opportunities exist in the way that institutions of higher education go about the business of environmental education. Innovation is in the wind. Students, faculty, and administrators from institutions across the United States and Canada are beginning to rethink campus operations in order to minimize or eliminate environmental impacts. Some campuses, such as the University of Georgia and the State University of New York at Buffalo, have organized task forces to develop detailed plans. And others are beginning to ask what the environmental crisis has to do with curricular and educational standards shaped by the dated assumptions that the world has no limits, that growth can continue forever, and that oil will always be priced at around $20 a barrel.

The contributors to this volume were not difficult to find. Six participated in a conference held at Northfield, Minnesota, in March 1991. The conference was the final event in a year-long study of food purchases initiated and conducted by the Meadowcreek Project on the campuses of Saint Olaf College and Carleton College. Other contributors came highly recommended through a small and growing grapevine of campus organizers, consultants, and environmental activists. All share a vision of institutions reshaped to better respond to the environmental challenges of this decade and beyond.

Common themes run throughout the work reported here. In one way

NEW DIRECTIONS FOR HIGHER EDUCATION, no. 77, Spring 1992   © Jossey-Bass Publishers

1

or another, many of the studies owe a debt to Amory and Hunter Lovins and the Rocky Mountain Institute for developing concepts such as *least-cost end-use analysis, energy efficiency, full-cost accounting*, and *rural development*. Most of these ideas can be readily adapted to the study of campus resource flows and related questions of investment and economic development. Most of the chapters describe attempts to apply more inclusive standards of efficiency to campus operations that require longer time horizons and more honest accounting of costs and benefits. This is partly a "how to do it" volume with practical suggestions. But it is, above all, an idea book designed to stimulate thinking about the evolution of institutions of higher education toward a twenty-first century agenda that must take account of the finiteness of the earth, the logic of systems and their interrelatedness, and an emerging ethic about our role as citizens of the biotic community and our responsibilities to future generations.

This is also a volume about institutional form and reform, which is to say, it describes a terrain littered with both good intentions and failures. But the stakes are different now. These chapters are about the response of higher education to the indisputable evidence of the deterioration of all major components of the biosphere. It is not too much to say that human survival is now in question. And how will those who presume to educate respond?

One final note on a small but significant matter. This volume is the first in the New Directions for Higher Education series to be printed on recycled paper. For that change we thank the editors and staff at Jossey-Bass. As with change on college and university campuses, small changes over a long enough time lead to a different destination.

David J. Eagan
David W. Orr
Editors

DAVID J. EAGAN holds degrees in biology and anthropology and is a doctoral candidate in the higher education program at the University of Wisconsin, Madison. He is project director for the Campus Environmental Stewardship Initiative.

DAVID W. ORR is professor of environmental studies at Oberlin College, Oberlin, Ohio. He is the author of Ecological Literacy: Education and the Transition to a Postmodern World *(State University of New York Press, 1991).*

Our greatest challenge lies in rethinking what kind of education is appropriate for a species whose standards of success threaten its ecological foundations.

The Problem of Education

David W. Orr

If today is a typical day on this planet, we will lose 145 square miles of rain forest, or about an acre-and-a-half each second. We will lose another 72 square miles of vegetation to encroaching deserts, the result of human mismanagement and overpopulation. We will lose between 40 and 250 species, most in tropical rain forests. Today the human population will increase by a quarter million. And today we will add twenty-seven hundred tons of chlorofluorocarbons to the atmosphere and fifteen million tons of carbon. Tonight the earth will be a little hotter, its soils and waters more acidic, and the fabric of life more threadbare. By the year's end, the numbers will be staggering; the total loss of rain forest will equal an area the size of the state of Washington, expanding deserts will equal the size of the state of West Virginia, and the global population will have risen by more than ninety million. By the year 2000 perhaps as much as 20 percent of the life forms that inhabited the earth in the year 1900 will be extinct (Brown and others, 1992). In short, many things on which our future health and prosperity depend are in dire jeopardy: the stability of the climate, the resilience and productivity of natural systems, the beauty of the natural world, and biological diversity.

Ecological destruction has been going on in one form or another for thousands of years, mostly done in ignorance of the long-term consequences. In contrast to earlier times, however, the results of ecological malfeasance now are often global and pose irreversible risks to our future. And we can no longer truthfully say that we do not know what we are doing. Environmental mismanagement is too often the work of the highly educated people with B.A.'s, B.S.'s, LL.B.'s, M.B.A.'s, and Ph.D.'s who, in the poet Gary Snyder's words, often "make unimaginably large sums of money,

NEW DIRECTIONS FOR HIGHER EDUCATION, no. 77, Spring 1992 © Jossey-Bass Publishers

people impeccably groomed, excellently educated at the best universities—male and female alike—eating fine foods and reading classy literature, while orchestrating the investment and legislation that ruin the world" (Snyder, 1990, p. 119).

When the actions of educated people "ruin the world," for whatever cause, it is time to ask what went wrong in their education. One answer, suggested by Elie Wiesel, is that modern education has too often emphasized theories, not values, abstraction rather than lived reality, answers instead of questions, and know-how rather than know-why (Wiesel, 1990). On balance, modern education has certainly better equipped us to dominate nature rather than dwell in harmony with it and to understand things in fragments rather than think broadly about systems and ecosystems. More of this kind of education will only compound our problems. This is not an argument for ignorance, but rather a statement that the worth of education must now be measured against the standards of decency and human survival—the issues looming so large before us in the decade of the 1990s and beyond.

The Challenge to Education

The crisis of the biosphere is symptomatic of a prior crisis of mind, perception, and heart. It is not so much a problem *in* education but a problem *of* education. The challenge before educators is that of developing in themselves and their students mindsets and habits that enable people to live sustainably on a planet with a biosphere. This crisis has relatively little to do with SAT scores, school budgets, or computer literacy, or even with our ability to compete in the world marketplace. It is rather about basic and mostly unstated assumptions that affect the ecological literacy and competence of students, faculty, and those charged with administration and oversight. Ultimately, the crisis of the biosphere is a test of our commitments, values, and foresight. For colleges and universities, this test has four parts.

First, it is a test of our beliefs about the purposes of education. Higher education is still more often than not justified on the grounds that it is a key to "success," which means upward mobility and higher lifetime earnings. These attributes, in turn, are crude but useful indicators of the amount of carbon that the graduate will redistribute from the subsurface of the earth to the atmosphere over a lifetime of consumption, travel, "enlightenment," and upward mobility. It is time to rethink the purposes of learning, knowledge, and research as if human longevity on earth really does matter.

Second, the crisis of the environment is a challenge to institutional routines and operational procedures. The common thesis in all of the studies reported in this volume is that the institutions purporting to induct students into responsible adulthood should themselves act responsibly toward the earth and all of its inhabitants. This thesis directs attention to the social and ecological costs of what comes into the campus—food, energy, water, materials—and what leaves in the form of wastes—organic matter, toxics, materials—and to the policies that govern purchasing, landscaping, architecture, transportation, and institutional investments. Until recently, campus resource flows were regarded as technical matters of institutional management, not problems of moral or even pedagogical concern. Institutions made decisions about what to buy and where to buy it on the basis of prices, which often did not include unassessed environmental and social costs. This practice often places institutions in the dubious position of undermining the quality of the world that their graduates will inherit.

Colleges and universities must learn to act responsibly in such matters not only because it is right to be responsible, but also because it is in their self-interest. The imaginative use of institutional buying and investment power can help build sustainable economies in the surrounding region, and these local economies may be related to the long-term health of the institution. A decade or two from now, for example, energy prices will rise sharply as a result of controls on acid rain and emissions of carbon dioxide. As these energy prices rise, the prices of everything from food to paper will rise as well. Institutions that have helped restore resilient regional economies will do better financially than will those still dependent on distant suppliers. Institutions that operate efficiently and reduce waste throughout their operations will do better still. And those drawing on regional suppliers, operating efficiently, and taking full advantage of natural services for energy, pest control, landscaping, and heating and cooling, for example, will do best of all. In other words, the economies of the institution and those of the surrounding region that grew apart in the era of cheap energy and externalized environmental costs will be brought closer together in a world of rising energy prices and environmental limits.

Third, the planetary crisis will test our creativity as educators. The crisis now unfolding around us calls into question old and comfortable pedagogical conventions about the disciplinary structure of knowledge, the separation of intellectual from experiential learning, and even how we think about intelligence. We have come to define education as intellectual mastery of fragmented and isolated subjects, most of which are far removed from daily experience. Consequently, for students the world of ideas has become increasingly abstract and remote from the reality of everyday life. The danger of abstract and analytical thinking carried to an extreme is that "we lose our sense of belonging to the world about us. . . . It divorces us from our own dispositions at the level where intellect and emotions fuse" (Gray, 1984, pp. 79, 85). The separation of intellect and practical experience has consequences for what one thinks about and how well one thinks about it. Most of the projects described in the following chapters involve students in one way or another. In the analysis of institutional resource flows, students learn a great deal about their institutions and about how the world works that they could not have learned otherwise. This is education of a high sort.

The study of institutional resource flows suggests a nontraditional pedagogy that involves students in matters that are direct, tangible, immediate, and consequential. In the food studies at Hendrix, Saint Olaf, and Carleton Colleges (Valen, this volume; Bakko and Woodwell, this volume) for example, staff members and college students analyzed food service invoices, studied farms and feedlots throughout the United States that supplied the campuses, and worked with local farmers to assess alternatives. Students participated in every step, all the way through the preparation of the proposals that went to the respective college administrations. In the process, students learned how their institutions worked; they learned about agriculture, economics, ecology, and ethics; and they learned that they were implicated in food service systems that were neither sustainable nor just. When their colleges adopted the proposals, they also learned that they could effect real change.

The analysis of campus resource flows also downscales global problems to a manageable size. Despair is the typical response to overwhelming problems such as global warming or the loss of biological diversity. Students need to know that global problems exist and that these problems threaten their future. But they also need to know how to solve problems, beginning at the institutional level. By making the institution a laboratory for the study and implementation of solutions, students learn how to analyze complex, multidisciplinary problems, how to formulate and compare alternatives, and how to transform institutions to fit the emerging realities of the next century. Instead of despair, students and faculty learn responsible optimism. Instead of learning that problems can only be solved by experts somewhere else, they learn that solutions can begin with the active and sometimes agitated participation of individuals in a campus community. Instead of dichotomies such as "good guys" versus "bad guys," students learn the arts of cooperation, aikido politics, and "getting to yes." Institutional administrators can also learn to see their institutions in a larger context and learn new ways to think through budgets that use methods such as "least-cost end-use analysis." They may also come to see their institutions as leverage points for helping to build environmentally and socially sustainable economies.

Beyond problems of resource flows, energy efficiency, closure of waste loops, recycling of paper and materials, elimination of unnecessary toxic materials on campus, and so forth, there are questions that concern the substance and process of education. The liberal arts, in a sense, have not been liberal enough. The time has come to rethink how the liberal arts can be measured against the yardstick of planetary sustainability. The damage to the earth sustained over the past 150 years through the process of industrialization will not be undone in our lifetimes, or even in those of our great grandchildren. The ozone layer will not recover its 1950 level for another 100 to 200 years. We will not bring carbon dioxide levels down to their preindustrial levels of 280 ppm for a century or longer, if then. Toxic wastes will last for thousands of years, radioactive wastes for hundreds of thousands of years. And the loss of biodiversity can never be undone. Still, we are learning something of the arts of healing, the *ecological design arts*. In this category, I include work now underway in sustainable agriculture, sustainable forestry, ecological engineering, restoration ecology, solar design, energy efficiency, ecological economics, and landscape design. These arts are not merely extensions of existing curricula but rather fundamentally new ways of seeing the human role in the natural world. For example, restoration ecology is a way of learning biology by putting biological systems back together again. Sustainable agriculture is agriculture patterned on natural processes. Ecological engineering involves the creation of ensembles of plants and animals as "living machines" to do what industrial technology can only do clumsily, expensively, and destructively. Ecological economics begins with "prices that tell the truth" about biotic impoverishment. Taken far enough, these and similar changes may enable educators and educational institutions to become healing agents for a damaged planet and a threatened humanity.

Finally, the decline in the habitability of the earth is a test of our commitment to Truth in its largest dimensions. According to the political theorist Glenn Tinder, "It is not truth as such that modern man has sought, but truth of a particular kind: truth that is verifiable and usable," driven by "the will to mastery" (Tinder, 1981, 116–117). What Tinder calls "humbling truth" is of a different sort, aimed toward health, justice, fairness, peace, and all of those things that tie us together in community—including the biotic community. Humbling truth has to do with wisdom and restraint, not technical fixes. Humbling truth would lead us to ask more often, "How much is enough?" and "For what purpose?" Those seeking truth of this sort know that ignorance is not a solvable problem, as Descartes assumed, but an inescapable and paradoxical given in the human condition. This recognition should inform all of our attempts to acquire knowledge and use it wisely.

Conclusion

The dawning awareness of the limits of the earth is a challenge to educators at every level everywhere. The knowledge and pedagogy necessary to subdue the earth is not entirely suitable to our becoming "plain member and citizen" of the biotic community (Leopold, 1966, p. 240). But signs of change in educational priorities and directions are now more evident than ever before. And no institutions in modern society are better able to catalyze the necessary transition than schools, colleges, and universities. They have access to the leaders of tomorrow, and through alumni, to the leaders of today. They have buying and investment power. They are widely respected; consequently, what they do matters to the wider public. And through faculty research and publication, they have a great impact on what people pay attention to. The question is not whether colleges and universities could help catalyze the transition to a sustainable society, but whether they have the vision and the courage to do so.

References

Brown, Lester, and others. *State of the World: 1992.* New York: Norton, 1992. (See also the 1990 and 1991 volumes.)

Gray, J. Glenn. *Rethinking American Education.* Middletown, Conn.: Wesleyan University Press, 1984.

Leopold, Aldo. *A Sand County Almanac.* New York: Ballantine, 1966.

Snyder, Gary. *The Practice of the Wild.* San Francisco: North Point Press, 1990.

Tinder, Glenn. *Against Fate: An Essay on Personal Dignity.* Notre Dame, Ind.: Notre Dame University Press, 1981.

Wiesel, Elie. Speech before the Global Forum in Moscow, January 1990.

DAVID W. ORR *is professor of environmental studies at Oberlin College, Oberlin, Ohio. He is the author of* Ecological Literacy: Education and the Transition to a Postmodern World *(State University of New York Press, 1991).*

Documentation of the full range of campus environmental impacts is a vital first step, but hard data do not ensure that change will be forthcoming in campus policy and practice.

Campus Environmental Audits: The UCLA Experience

April A. Smith, Robert Gottlieb

As a dozen students from the Graduate School of Architecture and Urban Planning at the University of California, Los Angeles (UCLA) and their faculty adviser sat around one day in 1988, discussing what kind of master's thesis they wanted to pursue, it became apparent that a division had emerged. One group of students wanted to undertake a study of the issues and problems associated with our "own backyard," the UCLA campus environment. The second group of students spoke of the importance of community-based research and worried that research more specifically focused on the campus environment would not be sufficiently oriented toward the "real world." There was a great deal of passion in the discussion from both sides: The community-oriented students cared deeply about the issues of environmental hazards and inequities facing poor and unrepresented communities around the country. The students advocating an environmental analysis of UCLA felt equally compelled to argue that a sense of responsibility had to begin with our own community, and that the campus environment for too long had been neglected and undisputed terrain. Although the discussion ultimately resulted in the formation of two different research projects, it established some common points of reference: Environmental issues are ubiquitous, they are often ignored in crucial arenas, and the engagement of these issues must begin at home—in those institutions where one works, resides, consumes, or goes to school.

The UCLA Study

The six students who decided to pursue an analysis of the campus environment quickly discovered that our "home"—UCLA—offered a significant

NEW DIRECTIONS FOR HIGHER EDUCATION, no. 77, Spring 1992 © Jossey-Bass Publishers

model in terms of both environmental problems and potential solutions. The largest of the nine University of California campuses, UCLA contains at least fifty thousand people, including thirty-four thousand students, who used the 411-acre campus on any given day. With a population and set of land uses and facilities similar to those of a small city, the university, situated in an affluent section of West Los Angeles, presented a case study of institutional environmental problems that reflect the process of contemporary environmental policy.

We decided to pursue, as the format of our research, an institutional environmental audit of the university, a process that included a comprehensive characterization of campus environmental issues, an analysis of the governance mechanisms and regulatory framework guiding campus policies, a review of practices at other universities and similar institutions, and a set of recommendations for improving current campus policies and programs. The research team specifically reviewed eleven key environmental issues at UCLA: the workplace environment; solid waste, hazardous waste, medical waste, and radioactive waste generation and disposal; air quality; storm water and waste water runoff and discharge; water and energy use; and procurement policies. The report's methodology included extensive interviews with UCLA management and staff personnel, review of existing legislation and regulatory policies affecting the university, and a comprehensive analysis of documents and published materials as well as original research such as a campus waste characterization study. The six-month research process culminated in the publication of the report *In Our Backyard: Environmental Issues at UCLA, Proposals for Change, and the Institution's Potential as a Model* (Brink and others, 1989).

UCLA, the study discovered, represents a microcosm of environmental problems. Activities are diverse, ranging from the university's research and educational functions to the infrastructure requirements for maintaining campus facilities. Like many of the largest campuses around the country, UCLA's numerous facilities and functions, including residence halls, food services, retail operations, maintenance operations, classrooms, offices, laboratories, art studios, and medical facilities, all have environmental impacts. The largest single difference from most municipalities and even broadly equivalent industrial or commercial operations is the approach that the university takes with respect to regulatory provisions initiated by local, state, and/or national agencies or from legislative mandates. To a great extent, the university seeks to exempt itself, sometimes successfully, from outside regulation, particularly at a local level. "The University of California," one administrator told us in 1988, "is like the Russian embassy. The city just can't tell us what to do."

Findings and Recommendations

For each issue area, the UCLA study reviewed the types and quantities of resources consumed and the amount of waste generated, evaluated the current programs in place, and proposed recommendations for improving environmental management. The findings of the audit reveal that the ecological impacts of an institution as large and diverse as UCLA are significant, as are the opportunities for change.

Workplace. In the area of the workplace environment, we identified a range of occupational hazards, from exposure to laboratory chemicals, airborne contaminants, and hazardous art materials and supplies, to pesticide use and activities associated with the physical plant and plant machinery. Safety policies and training programs were reviewed, and recommendations were made to expand safety procedures for those areas not traditionally identified as hazardous, such as art, architecture, and theater studios. These departments can contain potential hazards such as paints, solvents, and adhesives and may be subject to poor ventilation, thereby exacerbating indoor air quality problems. Suggested recommendations for improving the workplace environment included integrated pest management for indoor pest control and expanded nonsmoking policies.

Wastes and Hazards. The report analyzed the range of questions associated with the generation and disposal of solid, hazardous, medical, and radioactive wastes. We also conducted a waste characterization study as part of the research, which determined that over half of the university's solid waste was potentially recyclable, including a significant percentage of high-quality recyclables such as white ledger paper. At the same time, we discovered that no centralized campus recycling program existed; only a few voluntary programs established within different buildings or residences were in place due to the administration's skepticism and concerns about the aesthetic and fiscal viability of campuswide recycling. Instead, at the time we conducted the study, the vast majority of campus solid waste was landfilled. The university, moreover, saw itself as exempt from any city-based recycling program, arguing that the University of California Board of Regents was the appropriate rule-making authority. The report concluded that UCLA needed to develop a comprehensive, campuswide waste management strategy, based on a hierarchy of objectives, with source reduction requiring the greatest attention, followed by reuse (and composting, in particular) and recycling programs.

Hazardous waste, though less critical as a volume-based issue, nevertheless was a significant environmental concern given the range of sources and types of wastes involved. Like many campuses, UCLA's hazardous waste originates with laboratories, medical facilities, art studios, offices, cleaning and maintenance operations, asbestos removal, and vehicle maintenance. These sources generated more than one hundred tons of waste in 1988, according to university estimates. Most hazardous waste practices have been designed as a consequence of regulatory requirements, although a few, more proactive programs have been developed to reduce the volume of waste generated. The most striking area of innovation involves an effort, initiated by a chemistry professor and supported by the campus Office of

Instructional Development, to implement a microscale laboratory program in organic chemistry courses, a practice that reduces the quantity of chemicals used, thereby reducing costs both for purchase of chemicals as well as for waste disposal and improving potential laboratory safety and air quality problems. The report recommendations included a proposal both to expand microscale to other departments and to establish a comprehensive system for tracking the purchase and location of hazardous materials.

As the research institution with the largest licensed use of radioactive materials in California, UCLA generates a substantial quantity of low-level radioactive waste and is a major player in the effort to site in California a radioactive waste landfill facility. A number of strong radiation safety programs, tied largely to regulatory requirements, have been instituted, though the study also recommended further exploration in the area of potential reduction of wastes. UCLA is also one of the largest medical research and hospital facilities in the region and, consequently, a large generator of medical wastes, though any attempt to quantify such wastes is complicated by uncertainties in the definition of distinctive waste streams. The audit highlighted some emerging problems in the handling of medical wastes, such as potential toxic air emissions from incineration of medical wastes that contain plastics.

In the area of water pollution, UCLA, like other large institutions, contributes significantly to the problem both through discharges of wastewater into the overtaxed sewage treatment system of the city of Los Angeles and through unintentioned disposal of pollutants that may be washed through storm drains to the ocean. The audit estimated that UCLA's sewage flow constituted nearly .50 percent of all wastewater treated at the primary sewage treatment plant of Los Angeles, a significant amount for one institution. UCLA, however, has exempted itself from city-based sewer service fees and from city ordinances designed to limit increases in sewage flow. Additionally, wastewater flows have not been monitored to determine whether they are free of toxic pollutants stemming from improper toxic substance disposal practices. Improved water conservation practices and greater educational efforts regarding the use and disposal of toxic substances were proposed as part of the overall analysis of campus wastewater management.

Air Quality. In a region with the nation's worst air quality, UCLA was identified by the regional South Coast Air Quality Management District as the tenth largest emitter of carbon monoxide in 1987. Emissions sources included fleet and private vehicles as well as stationary sources such as campus steam plants and paint booths. UCLA's award-winning ride-sharing program, viewed as a model for other institutions, has reduced the number of vehicle trips to campus, although the continued construction of new parking facilities, a major financial undertaking by the university partially designed to increase its attractiveness for recruitment purposes, conflicts with the goals of the ride-sharing program.

Water Use. At the time of the study, UCLA was the eighth largest water consumer in the city of Los Angeles, which was then experiencing the beginnings of what has turned out to be a deep and protracted drought throughout the region and the state. Similar to its stated policy with respect to city-initiated, mandatory measures for solid waste and wastewater management, UCLA exempted itself from the city's drought ordinance, though administrators stated that the campus would seek to comply with the then voluntary reductions of 10 percent that had been proposed for other users in the city. Up to the time of the study, the school's water consumption, reflecting in part a growth in campus population, had been increasing over the past decade, though certain water conservation measures had been initiated, such as the installation of low-flush toilets in some buildings. The report recommended the expansion of these and other water conservation measures, including systematic leak detection and the introduction of drought-tolerant landscaping.

Energy Use. In the area of energy use, the audit identified UCLA through utility records as the third largest consumer of electricity in the city of Los Angeles. According to our analysis, the university's energy management program, while effective for specific projects developed primarily for cost savings purposes, lacked comprehensive planning and innovation. Nor had the university's own significant research and educational resources related to energy analysis been employed, a situation similar to most campuses around the country. The report recommended the systematic use of such resources and the development of innovative programs such as daylighting (design techniques that maximize the use of natural lighting) and passive solar heating and cooling in new construction tied to UCLA's ambitious capital projects expansion program.

Procurement Practices. A review of university procurement policies revealed that UCLA, and indeed the entire University of California system, could play a significant role in conservation by purchasing recycled and environmentally sound products. This practice would in turn help create and sustain markets for materials and products such as recycled paper, organic produce, and nontoxic cleaning supplies. During the research, we also discovered that the University of California system was actively opposing proposed legislation mandating a purchasing preference for recycled paper in university contracts. The report recommended a number of changes in university procurement policies as a way to incorporate environmental criteria in purchasing decisions.

Report Summary. In terms of the overall analysis of university policies and activities, the report identified key factors that have shaped the decision-making process as they relate to the wide variety of campus environmental impacts and issues. These factors include financial and other resource constraints and priorities, regulatory and policy gaps, questions of image and aesthetics, and the preference for large-scale, technically oriented solutions such as a cogenerating plant (with its cost savings and reduced energy use, but increased air emissions) rather than more labor-intensive, behaviorally oriented approaches such as "turn-off-the-light" stickers to conserve energy and source-separation-based recycling. At the same time, the failure to apply environmentally oriented university research and education within the university framework itself had significant implications in a number of key arenas such as energy use, toxics use, and waste generation and disposal. This failure also inhibited the development of a systematic framework for addressing, and reduced the level of innovation involving, environmental issues within the institution.

The report concluded that significant environmental issues did need to be addressed, many of them related to the university's size and multiple land uses and functions, as well to the university's own policy-making process. Moreover, by drawing on resources available within the campus community, identifying sources of financial and other forms of support both inside and outside the university structure, and developing comprehensive and systemwide environmental planning in conjunction with other strategic planning efforts, UCLA also had the potential of becoming an institutional model for environmental change.

Going Public

Even prior to the report's public release, In Our Backyard became the subject of much interest and some controversy. An article in the Los Angeles Times (Roark, 1989) ran shortly prior to the report's publication and drew a sharp response from the university administration, which also objected to the substantial press coverage that followed, including reports by the New York Times, National Public Radio, CNN, the Associated Press, the Chronicle of Higher Education, and numerous local television and radio stations. Aside from general public relations considerations, university administrators were particularly concerned about any impact that the report's release might have on the university's long-range development plans, which included significant campus expansion involving at that time upward of four million square feet of new campus buildings.

The university administration's objections centered around two primary issues. First, university officials strongly criticized what they perceived to be the report's findings, arguing that the findings portrayed the university in a negative light and that the particular numbers cited—such as third largest electricity user or eighth largest water user in the city—were exclusively a function of the university's size and bore no direct relation to policy considerations. Second, that the report was a *student* product and yet received a seemingly unprecedented degree of media attention was disturbing to the administration, a situation further exacerbated by our initial release of a draft copy of the report to the Los Angeles Times.

After the initial controversy began to subside, the university administration and the Associated Students organization at UCLA (which, with its $80 million annual budget, is responsible for food services, campus stores, and the campus student union) pursued sharply different approaches to the report's recommendations. Associated Students, which placed one of our student authors on its board, reviewed those proposals from *In Our Backyard* that were applicable to its facilities and activities and, in turn, initiated a series of new policies and programs partly in response to that review. These included a reusable mug program and a number of other solid waste reduction or reuse initiatives, a new procurement policy, and an improved recycling program. In contrast to these responses and the recommendations of the report, the UCLA administration developed a solid waste program based on a single-container collection system and a mixed-waste recycling effort undertaken at a transfer station off campus. Although, in a widespread promotional campaign, the university claimed exceptionally high "recycling" rates of up to 70 percent, it included as part of its recycling numbers that part of the waste earmarked for incineration, despite recently enacted state legislation excluding incineration from the definition of waste diversion.

Consequences of the Report

Soon after the release of *In Our Backyard,* staff from the Earth Day 1990 project approached us about developing a model audit as the centerpiece for the national Earth Day student campaign. This request coincided with a number of inquiries from administrators, staff, faculty, and students at other campuses about the findings of the report and its availability. As a result, we constructed a campus environmental audit as a guide, consisting of a fifty-page summary of the methods used in the *In Our Backyard* study and a discussion on how to pursue this type of undertaking at other campuses. The model audit, which was distributed to over one thousand campuses in the United States and abroad and was successfully completed by nearly one hundred schools as part of their Earth Day activities, has since become a widely recognized blueprint for instituting campus environmental change. Both our original audit and *In Our Backyard* have also been used as curricular material at a number of different campuses, while the model audit has been expanded for publication (Smith, forthcoming) to include such issues as campus investment policies, research activities, environmental education, and land use policies.

One of the most striking consequences of the report has been the integration of the audit project into the programmatic work of the Student Environmental Action Coalition (SEAC). SEAC, formed in 1988 and headquartered in North Carolina, is a national environmental network for college and high school students, focusing on such issues as corporate and university accountability in the environmental area. The growth of SEAC since 1988 has been exceptional, making it the largest student environmental organization in the country, with an international network and several successful annual conventions that attract a geographically diverse and large number of student participants.

Since it was first introduced in 1990, the campus environmental audit has continued to be a powerful tool for bringing about environmental change at colleges, universities, and high schools across the country and for providing students with a vehicle for applying knowledge learned in the classroom to their immediate campus experience. At Lansing Community College in Michigan, for example, students conducted a solid waste characterization study, with a particular emphasis on organic material, as part of the course requirements for a statistics class. In addition to collecting data that supported a compelling argument for a campus composting program, the audit was used as a tool for learning statistical methodology, a process usually reserved to the traditional classroom setting.

The audit has also been instrumental in opening up lines of communication between students and administrators about campus environmental issues, as well as in establishing and institutionalizing campus environmental programs and expanding the range of possibilities for change. At Oklahoma Baptist University, in Shawnee, students used the audit to expand their efforts beyond a recycling program by establishing an appointed position on the student council for a campus environmental commissioner. The commissioner is responsible for creating an annual task force on the campus environment to review possible avenues for change. As a result of these activities, the university was recently successful in attracting matching funds from the U.S. Department of Energy for designing and implementing campus energy efficiency programs. In these and other examples, the audit has demonstrated that the traditional gaps between student activists and campus authorities can be bridged by providing students with the knowledge and skills needed to become credible players in the eyes of administrators. Along with projects such as the National Wildlife Federation's Cool It! project and organizations such as SEAC, the audit has helped create a new framework around campus environmental issues, in part by enabling students and campus administrators to shift from confrontational to cooperative relationships.

In Our Backyard in Perspective

The *In Our Backyard* experience, from the original research and findings to the varying responses and their aftermath, offers some rich and compelling lessons. That students, albeit highly motivated, graduate students, capably undertook a study of this magnitude and complexity and developed a coherent policy analysis and set of recommendations was an empowering series of events. It suggests, for example, some of the early research efforts of "Nader's Raiders," many of whom were students or recent graduates, who, in turn, pursued crucial analyses of pollution-based issues in the late 1960s and early 1970s that ultimately resulted in significant policy initiatives. Moreover, this student-based research on the university-environment relationship brought together two very powerful and compelling arenas for action: (1) the university, with its crucial research and teaching functions and its substantial impacts on the community and the environment and (2) the environment, in an institutional setting, where the need and the possibilities for change are immediate and pressing.

At the outset of the *In Our Backyard* study, the idea of a university environmental analysis seemed more idiosyncratic than structurally relevant. In perspective, it now seems clear that in both content and process the UCLA study demonstrated not only that universities, as a function of their size and the nature of their activities, have environmental significance but that their policies are critical as well. Universities, like many other institutions that are often viewed as outside the framework of environmental analysis, are environmental players; their decision making is part of the context of identifying problems and seeking solutions. A study by students of that university role, moreover, needs to be seen as central to the educational process; the practice of thinking and acting critically is also about knowing, understanding, and addressing the issues of one's own backyard. Today, thanks in part to the example of *In Our Backyard*, the opportunity to recreate and expand on that experience is now available at campuses throughout the country.

References

Brink, Tamra, Dill, Jennifer, Holmblad, Gretchen, Little, Bryce, Sadun, Anita Glazer, and Smith, April. *In Our Backyard: Environmental Issues at UCLA, Proposals for Change, and the Institution's Potential as a Model.* Los Angeles: Graduate School of Architecture and Urban Planning, University of California, Los Angeles, 1989.

Roark, Anne. "UCLA Identifies a Major Source of Pollution—Itself." *Los Angeles Times,* June 15, 1989.

Smith, April. *The Campus Environmental Audit: A Guide to Creating Campus Environmental Change.* Venice, Calif.: Living Planet Press, in press.

APRIL A. SMITH *is a consultant and environmental planner in Los Angeles. She was a member of the research team that wrote* In Our Backyard *and is the author of* The Campus Environmental Audit: A Guide to Creating Campus Environmental Change.

ROBERT GOTTLIEB *was faculty supervisor for the students who wrote* In Our Backyard *and currently teaches environmental policy in the Urban Planning Program at the University of California, Los Angeles. He is a co-author of* War on Waste: Can America Win Its Battle with Garbage? *(Island Press, 1989).*

In 1990, the president of Tufts University became the first leader of a major university to establish environmental education and protection as institutional priorities.

Environmental Literacy and Action at Tufts University

Sarah Hammond Creighton, Anthony D. Cortese

We can no longer depend only on professionals in government, industry, academia, and public interest groups to address the complexities of environmental protection. Instead, all members of society need to understand how the environment is important to their own existence and quality of life. We each need to have the knowledge, the tools, and the will to conduct our daily lives and professions in ways that minimize our personal adverse impacts. The Tufts Environmental Literacy Institute (TELI) and Tufts CLEAN! (Cooperation, Learning, and Environmental Awareness Now!) are two programs that try to address this need.

TELI is a faculty development program aimed at making the connection between a wide range of academic disciplines and the natural environment in order to produce environmentally literate Tufts graduates. Tufts CLEAN! complements this effort by helping staff and students understand and reduce adverse environmental impacts of business conducted at Tufts. This chapter describes the goals and approaches taken by these two unique programs.

Tufts Environmental Literacy Institute

In 1990, Tufts President Jean Mayer announced a goal that all students graduating from Tufts be environmentally literate. This literacy calls for students to develop an awareness and understanding of the importance of the natural environment and the effects of human activities on it, as well as an appreciation for the complexity of this interaction. With initial support from the Allied Signal Foundation, and later from Union Carbide and

NEW DIRECTIONS FOR HIGHER EDUCATION, no. 77, Spring 1992 © Jossey-Bass Publishers

the Environmental Protection Agency (EPA), TELI was established at the Center for Environmental Management (CEM) to provide educators from a wide range of disciplines with tools to incorporate environmental issues into existing and new courses, and, ultimately, to provide students with a foundation for evaluating difficult environmental issues in the context of their professions and their lives.

Summer Workshops. TELI operates on the premise that humans and the environment are interconnected and that the incorporation of these connections into the teaching of all disciplines is one way to engender environmental literacy. The institute's central feature is a two-week intensive workshop in which a multidisciplinary group of faculty comes together to learn about environmental literacy. The workshop is designed to increase environmental knowledge and provide a forum for discussing how this information can meet the goals of specific courses. Environmental specialists from academia, government, industry, and public interest groups lead workshop sessions and present the science, management, and policy issues associated with topics such as solid and hazardous wastes, global climate change, health risk, and environmental economics. A member of what was formerly the Supreme Soviet, a Korean development economist, an Indian university president, and a Brazilian university faculty member joined Tufts specialists in conducting the 1991 program.

In 1990, our first year, TELI worked with twenty-five Tufts faculty members who attended the workshop and incorporated the teaching of environmental issues into mechanical engineering, economics, history, international diplomacy, drama, sociology, and chemistry curricula. In 1991, forty-five faculty members from Tufts and ten other universities, including universities in Brazil and Canada, participated in the program.

Some universities have approached environmental literacy by offering elective courses on environmental topics. The University of Northern Iowa, in Cedar Falls, even requires that all students take Environment, Technology, and Society, a core environmental issues course (Clausen, 1989). In contrast, TELI provides resources for faculty who integrate environmental issues into their existing courses. In this way, students get repeated exposure to these topics and opportunities to make connections between environmental controversies and issues from the core subject matter. Tufts also offers a variety of specific environmental courses and degree programs for students who seek to study the issues in depth. Clearly, a combination of strategies is needed to ensure environmental literacy.

Environmental Issues Across the Curriculum. After the summer workshop, TELI faculty revise their curricula to integrate environmental issues and perspectives and then teach the revised courses in the following academic year. Revised curricula are reviewed by other TELI faculty and made available to other universities as part of a larger strategy to extend the influence of TELI programs. The resulting course revisions most often take one of three formats. The first uses an environmental context to teach a concept or a skill. The second involves expansion of a problem-solving exercise to include influences from or effects on the environment. The third uses environmental topics to show the relevance of the subject matter or to make the existing course material more interesting.

For example, a drama professor used the environment as a theme for personal storytelling, acting, and selected readings. Two civil engineering professors modified their courses in geotechnology, soil mechanics, and foundation engineering to use environmental problems such as landfills, sludge disposal, and waste containment and cleanup along with more traditional examples such as dam building. A Spanish professor revised six courses required for a major in Spanish to include environmental readings from Spain and Latin America and to make environmental issues the subjects of paper topics and debates.

Improving the TELI Model. We are in the process of evaluating TELI and its effectiveness. Faculty participants have found educational value in the summer workshops and are enthusiastic about the opportunity to explore complex, intellectually challenging issues with colleagues from a variety of disciplines. They report that students find the revised courses interesting and stimulating. But a single workshop may not be sufficient to fully support this effort to engender environmental literacy. TELI faculty tell us that they need continuing support through specialized workshops, educational materials such as case studies, and mechanisms for keeping in touch with colleagues at Tufts and elsewhere.

Long-Term Goals. In addition to perpetuating and improving TELI at Tufts, we hope to help other universities establish environmental literacy programs unique to their respective needs. In addition, we hope that educators in government and the private sector incorporate these issues into their own specific curricula. We plan to assist in the efforts of establishing and evaluating these new programs by cosponsoring workshops and long-term partnerships among institutions that include historically black colleges and universities, universities in Eastern Europe, Canada, and developing countries, and government and industry. Our goal is to work with five hundred faculty members from Tufts and other audiences over the next five years. At this level of participation, an estimated seventy-five thousand to one-hundred thousand students will receive broad, continuing, and repeated exposure to environmental issues over this period in the context of their regular disciplinary studies.

Tufts CLEAN!

TELI is only a part of a comprehensive approach to teaching Tufts students about environmental problems and their complex solutions. Universities are good at studying the environmental impacts of others, but they often fail to recognize and reduce their own impacts. In mid-1990, EPA funded Tufts CLEAN! in order to make a difference at Tufts. Our goal is to create a set of models for pollution prevention that will lead to a reduction of the adverse local, regional, and global environmental impacts of Tufts's own activities.

Participation at All Levels. Active support from the administration is essential to the success of a program such as CLEAN! (Cortese and Creighton, 1991). The Tufts CLEAN! Coordinating Committee, composed of senior vice presidents and deans representing all the schools, was formed to keep top management involved. This group oversees the project, establishes policy, and reviews recommendations. A working advisory board, representing operations staff, faculty, and students, sets priorities, acts as a sounding board for project ideas, and facilitates environmental efforts throughout the Tufts community. We are currently in the process of forming several specific task forces to address issues such as dining service and transportation in depth. These task forces are useful in building relationships and involving key people in the project.

Role of Staff. In this effort, staff from Tufts CLEAN!, located at CEM, act as catalysts for change, often generating ideas, networking, or serving as technical assistants. We are finding that often we spend as much time developing a relationship and understanding how things operate as we do researching the technical details of a given project. In some ways, we operate like the environmental department of a corporation, yet, in other ways, we are like volunteer consultants. Along the way we have tried to be diplomatic by working cooperatively with university personnel, involving them in our research of alternatives and assessments of feasibility. We believe that successful projects become institutionalized, and we work hard to give credit to those outside of CEM who play ongoing roles.

Understanding Our Environmental Impacts. Initial research revealed that Tufts has a significant impact on its environment. Nearly eight thousand students and thirty-five hundred faculty and staff live at, or commute daily to, one of our three campuses. Hazardous chemicals and radioactive isotopes are used and generated in the process of teaching and conducting research in biology, chemistry, fine arts, and medicine. Large amounts of energy are expended in heating and cooling buildings, heating water, providing lighting, and operating office machines.

Initially, we planned to conduct a comprehensive environmental audit of our activities and their impacts. We made flow diagrams showing how materials passed into and out of Tufts and proposed to quantify the amounts and the environmental effects of each of the hundreds of items in these diagrams. However, as we began the audit, it was soon obvious that "fifty simple things" really numbered five hundred or five thousand, and many were not simple at all. As a result, we decided that a comprehensive university audit would not in itself be effective in understanding and overcoming the status quo and other barriers to change. It is more effective to engage targeted university personnel in the process of implementing change, rather than in data collection alone. We decided to examine specific topics in depth and effect change in these areas. We are, however, targeting the university's central administration building for a comprehensive audit. In this effort, building occupants, working with Tufts CLEAN!, will identify needs, develop a specific action plan for the building, and implement the initiatives. We hope that the choice of this building will demonstrate Tufts's commitment to environmental stewardship while helping us to refine materials and a methodology suited to administrative buildings.

Understanding the Issues. To improve our understanding of university operations and decision making at Tufts, we held interviews with a variety of university personnel, including the directors of buildings and grounds, food services, purchasing, housing, student affairs, safety, and risk management. We also interviewed professors, department chairs, finance managers, and students. These meetings were important opportunities to introduce Tufts CLEAN! to the university community, determine the nature and extent of environmental protection efforts already underway, gather data on our environmental impacts, and gauge the level of interest. The interviews generated more qualitative information than quantitative, but they proved to be a valuable source of background information.

The bulk of the interviews took place in the six months following Earth Day 1990. At every turn, we were encouraged by people's willingness to cooperate and their enthusiasm for the issues, surprised to find that many initiatives had been undertaken, and sobered by the complexity of annually working with and educating over eleven thousand employees and students. We found that recycling was the overwhelming focus of people's participation in environmental protection. We heard frequent complaints about inadequate control of the heating systems, resulting in conditions of excessive heat or cold. Fiscal constraints affected most departments but provided motivation for existing efforts to improve efficiency. We asked for suggestions and found that there were plenty of opportunities to reduce environmental impacts in each building and department and in the university overall. In addition, we came to understand that existing ways of doing things evolve over long periods in response to complex sets of problems.

Setting Priorities. During the course of our interviews, it soon became obvious that many more projects needed attention than we could undertake at once. Our advisory board and some initial student work identified the need for an environmental policy, but we had a difficult time narrowing priorities beyond the broad topics of transportation, resource conservation, solid waste, and hazardous materials. In order to focus our attention on specific projects, we developed a list of criteria for selecting our work areas: (1) degree of environmental improvement, (2) potential savings, (3) ease of implementation, (4) length of time for results to be realized ("early returns"), (5) visibility and educational potential, and (6) connection to existing university goals and projects.

The Tufts CLEAN! projects undertaken in the first year reflect a combination of these criteria. The energy and transportation initiatives of CLEAN! offer opportunities to reduce some of Tufts's largest contributions to air pollution and emission of greenhouse effect gases. Our work with dining services is a direct response to that department's enthusiasm and willingness to act and provides high visibility for our actions. Other strategies, such as ECOlympics and efforts to promote the reuse of office paper, are visible and participatory opportunities to cut university costs. All of our projects demonstrate the need for commitment and the need for environmental literacy of students and staff alike.

Developing an Environmental Policy. Creation of a university environmental policy was one of our first priorities. Under the direction of the CLEAN! program, Tufts established a university environmental policy (see Exhibit 3.1), signed by President Mayer in April 1991. The policy, one of the first of its kind at a major university, was developed by representatives from the faculty, students, staff, and administration and drew heavily on policy statements from a number of U.S. corporations. It is unique in that it provides guidance to curriculum and research activities as well as to university operations.

Implementation of the policy over the years will help us achieve environmental literacy and minimize the adverse impacts of Tufts's activities on the environment. A number of Tufts CLEAN! projects illustrate how the general statements of the policy have been translated into action.

Reducing Solid Waste. Solid waste issues seem to be foremost in people's minds, although solid waste disposal may not necessarily result in the most pressing environmental impacts. Many university functions, including buildings and grounds, dining services, and purchasing, offer significant and tangible opportunities to reduce waste. Much has already been done in a variety of departments, and Tufts CLEAN! is documenting their progress and broadening these efforts to include waste reduction and use of alternative products.

Reduction and Reuse. We found that bona fide efforts for solid waste source reduction at Tufts and other universities are few. Restrictions on postering for student events, conversion to washable dishware, and refills of laser printer cartridges are common examples. Dartmouth and Brown universities make extensive use of electronic mail systems, since most students have computers that are hooked into the central system, but the effect on aggregate paper or electricity use has not been measured. At Tufts and elsewhere a deposit system provides a reusable alternative to plastic bags in the book store, and discounts are offered to beverage patrons who bring their own mugs.

Since newspaper recycling markets are glutted at this time, we investi-

Exhibit 3.1. Tufts University Environmental Policy

We, the Tufts University community, affirm our belief that university faculty, staff, and students have a responsibility to take a leadership role in conducting activities as responsible stewards of the physical environment and using educational activities to promote environmental awareness, local action, and global thinking.

In our university functions, Tufts University will strive to
conserve natural resources and support their sustainable use;
conduct affairs in a manner that safeguards the environmental health and safety of students, faculty, staff, and communities;
reduce the use of toxic substances and the generation of wastes and promote strategies to reuse and recycle those wastes that cannot be avoided; and purchase renewable, reusable, recyclable, and recycled materials.
In our education and research missions, Tufts University will strive to
foster an understanding of and a responsibility for the physical environment;
ensure that individuals are knowledgeable about the environmental and health issues that affect their disciplines;
encourage environmental research;
conduct research and teaching in an environmentally responsible way; and
provide a forum for the open flow of information among governments, international organizations, industry, and academia to discuss and study environmental issues and their relationship to other social issues.

In our student and employee relations, Tufts University will strive to delineate individual responsibility and guide action for ensuring safety and minimizing adverse environmental impacts in the implementation of this policy.

Tufts will consider full compliance with the law to be the minimally acceptable standard and will exercise whatever control is reasonable and necessary to avoid harm to public health and the environment, whether or not such control is required by regulations.

Tufts will initiate, promote, and conduct programs that fully implement this policy throughout the university and the global community.

---

gated the practice of using shredded old newspapers as bedding for animals at the Tufts University School of Veterinary Medicine. Unfortunately, shredded newspaper was not satisfactory since it interfered with proper operation of the animal hospital's ventilation and drainage systems. Conditions for research animals are closely regulated by research protocol, and the animal researchers were reluctant to risk changes in experimental conditions.

Tufts CLEAN! has been pushing the use of "precycle pads." These notepads are made by the university print shop in full, half, or quarter sheet sizes from sheets of paper used on one side that are "padded" with a nonhazardous cement. At CEM, precycle pads have saved us money and have helped our progress toward the goal of recycling paper only after it has been used on both sides.

Recycling. We are asked about our recycling program so often that we have concluded that successful recycling may be a precursor to the success of other programs. This special status may be due to the fact that recycling is highly visible, easy to understand, and participatory in nature. Office paper and newspaper recycling programs have been underway for two years at the Tufts Medford Campus, run largely by student volunteers working with buildings and grounds. The student effort had been autonomous until the university hired a resource coordinator to oversee the contracts, markets, collection, and containers for recycling. The coordinator, a Tufts graduate, is working to expand the recycling program to include an estimated twenty tons of cans and one hundred tons of corrugated cardboard annually. These efforts have been invaluable in engaging over 150 student recycling volunteers and bolstering enthusiasm for environmental efforts universitywide.

Composting. Until recently, the yard and food wastes from Tufts Medford campus were landfilled with other solid waste, although a new state law prohibits that practice. Tufts CLEAN! worked with students in a TELI course to conduct a cost-benefit analysis of yard waste composting and then helped the grounds department identify a workable strategy. As a result, ninety tons of leaves from fall 1991 were composted at a site near campus, with a cost savings of $1,500. In addition, a graduate student is testing several food waste composting techniques to gather data and demonstrate the feasibility of a larger-scale project. The resulting compost will be used on a community vegetable garden located at Tufts.

Reduction of Impacts Through Purchasing. Universities have tremendous power as consumers. At the same time, central purchasing systems have the authority to standardize product selections. This purchasing power and standardization offer important opportunities to affect markets and make sound, environmentally sensitive choices. The purchasing department at Tufts has already taken steps to reduce environmental impacts associated with some of the products that it buys. Examples include standardization of vehicles to ensure lower gas mileage, bulk purchases, promotion of recycled paper, and purchase of low-flow washing machines. Tufts CLEAN! is assisting in the development of procedures to evaluate the environmental impacts of products and to educate Tufts personnel about "green" alternatives. The dining committee, described below, is beginning to consider specific ways that the bidding process for food and supplies can include specific recyclability, recycled content of packaging, and local suppliers.

Reduction of Impacts of Dining. Tufts CLEAN! is spearheading a working group made up of students, dining personnel, and development staff to plan and implement strategies to reduce, reuse, and recycle dining's solid wastes. As a result, nearly three tons of corrugated cardboard have been recycled weekly since December 1991, and unbleached paper bags are now being used. Opportunities to improve energy efficiency are targeted for spring 1992. Student projects, modeled after those undertaken at Hendrix, Saint Olaf, and Carleton colleges (see Valen, this volume; Bakko and Woodwell, this volume), are now planned to investigate the environmental costs of foods and to develop proposals to work cooperatively with local farmers.

Reducing Energy Consumption. Tufts has three principal types of energy use: electricity, water and space heating (and cooling), and transportation. Energy production and use are major causes of the pollution generated by the university. We are evaluating efficiency and alternative energy options using life-cycle cost analyses and comparisons of current and estimated future costs where possible. In addition, we are exploring ways to combine technology with changes in institutional policy and individual behavior.

Electricity. On its three campuses combined, Tufts uses forty-four million kilowatt-hours of electricity each year. Improved electrical efficiency can reduce the amount of carbon dioxide and air toxics produced by Tufts. The region's electrical utilities offer generous rebates as incentives for improved efficiency. Owing to the rapid payback that these projects can yield, the buildings and grounds departments on all three campuses have used these rebates to defray the cost of retrofitting lamps, ballasts, daylight and occupancy sensors, pumps, and motors. The net effect of these changes can be enhanced by combining one-for-one retrofits with removals of unneeded lights, a measure that is often overlooked.

In contrast to the hands-on nature of recycling, individuals are more removed from the generation of electricity, its consequences, and payment of the bills, which may partly explain why there is less willingness to turn off lights that are not in use than there is to recycle. At Tufts, office lights are typically left on when professors or other staff are out, whether in class or at meetings, to indicate that they are dutifully on campus. There is also a widely held myth that the practice of switching lights on and off reduces their burn life; but while repeated switching shortens the total hours that bulbs will burn, their useful life can be increased and replacement costs delayed by keeping them off when they are not needed (Carriere and Rea, 1988).

Heating. Tufts uses oil and natural gas to heat buildings and water. The majority of buildings are old and have central controls that do not evenly regulate heat and are expensive to replace. Insulation and storm window projects have been undertaken by the physical plant in a few buildings, and opportunities to down-size air conditioners in buildings where lighting retrofits result in less heat gain are under consideration. Tufts CLEAN! is examining opportunities for solar water heating in the gymnasium and in the large animal hospital. Engineering students involved in a TELI course explored alternative energy options for several buildings and made recommendations for wind and solar projects.

Individuals' Contributions to Efficiency. Tufts is holding an ECOlympics during the school year 1991–1992, in which residents of residential halls, and possibly other university buildings, compete to reduce electricity and water use and contamination of recyclables in their buildings. Bonus points are awarded for responding to our environmental survey, for attending environmental workshops, and for using reusable mugs in the take-out dining cafeterias. This is a joint project of buildings and grounds, the student environmental group, residential life, and Tufts CLEAN!

Transportation. The 1990 Clean Air Act classifies the Boston area's air quality as severe, and it is well documented that transportation is a major contributor to this problem. We know that the average round-trip commute to our Medford campus is twenty-seven miles and that few staff use public transportation. We are developing strategies to reduce the consequences of campus travel activities by targeting a combination of institutional policy, individual behavior changes, and technology in five major areas: (1) commuter ride sharing, (2) ride sharing for university business, (3) university and public transportation systems, (4) university vehicle fleet, and (5) university policies and facilities. We hope to pilot-test these strategies in some or all of these areas in order to reduce Tufts's contributions to local air pollution, global warming, and the northeast region's dependence on petroleum.

Reducing Hazards. Five graduate students in the Hazardous Materials Management Program participated in Tufts CLEAN! research in summer 1990 by focusing on management and disposal practices in several departments that generate hazardous waste on the main campus. They identified opportunities to improve handling, training, and disposal practices. The group's oral presentation of results was attended by nearly fifty people and generated a lively dialogue. This report has been used as the foundation for further research by Tufts CLEAN! on issues associated with policy development and hazardous material management on campus. Development of a university environmental policy that applies to hazardous materials and improvement of disposal of photographic chemical wastes are two of the recommendations that already have been implemented. In spring 1992, Tufts CLEAN! is holding a series of focus group interviews to determine problems of hazardous material management faced by faculty.

The student project helped us learn that student involvement in the examination of hazardous materials may be problematic. We did not anticipate the sensitivity of the issues or properly advise university personnel prior to student interviews, nor did we clarify how the findings would be used. University personnel who were interviewed by students assumed that their comments were for internal use only, while the students assumed that their final document would be made public. Subsequent reports by students have avoided these problems by using fictitious names and locations for the situations examined.

Future Directions for TELI and Tufts CLEAN!

TELI and Tufts CLEAN! work complementarily to educate students, staff, and faculty. But the processes of developing environmental literacy and reducing environmental impacts take time. Over the next five years, we plan to broaden our goals for reducing impacts and to develop better strategies for achieving these goals. This process must be embraced by all parts of the university if it is to be completely successful. Toward this end, we will continue to establish short-term programs and initiatives. In addition to specific actions, we hope to incorporate environmental accountability as a key consideration in long-range university planning.

Also, one of our central objectives is to share the lessons of Tufts CLEAN! with other campuses. In the next year, we plan to spend more time documenting our experiences and working with others to determine the applicability of our programs in different circumstances.

Conclusions

The fact that the day-to-day operations of a university result in significant environmental impacts makes the university setting an ideal laboratory in which to explore new ways to reduce hazards, improve efficiency, reuse and recycle wastes, and develop incentives for institutionalizing environmental change. Because the environment provides the basis for life and is a major determinant of the quality of life, it must be a fully integrated and prominent part of all education. At Tufts, we are not waiting for a concerted national or international strategy but are instead taking steps on our own to ensure that an appreciation and understanding of the issues occur in the context of each discipline and in the process of living, eating, studying, and working at the university.

In implementing TELI and Tufts CLEAN!, we are learning that change is difficult and often slow. We are constantly relearning the importance of including the stakeholders in the process right from the beginning, identifying the right decision makers, and giving credit where it is due. All the while, we remain convinced that institutions and individuals must be motivated by more than economics to take action within their own walls or lives if we are to have a future that can sustain our needs.

References

Carriere, Louis A., and Rea, Mark S. "Economics of Switching Fluorescent Lamps." *IEEE Transactions on Industry Applications,* 1988, 24 (3), 370–379.

Clausen, Bernard L. "Mainstreaming Environmental Literacy." *Journal of Soil and Water Conservation,* 1989, 44 (6), 557–559.

Cortese, Anthony D., and Creighton, Sarah Hammond. "The Greening of American Universities." *Journal of the Association of Governing Boards of Universities and Colleges*, 1991, 33 (2), 24–29.

SARAH HAMMOND CREIGHTON *is the project manager for Tufts* CLEAN! *in Medford, Massachusetts. Previously, she examined environmental management practices of small businesses and managed research projects for an economic development consultant.*

ANTHONY D. CORTESE *is dean of environmental programs at Tufts University and program director for the Tufts Environmental Literacy Institute. He was the founding director for the Center for Environmental Management and served as the commissioner for the Massachusetts Department of Environmental Protection for six years.*

Campus energy programs can reduce costs, improve environmental quality, and provide a valuable educational experience for students.

Campus Energy Management Programs

Morris A. Pierce

For several decades, inexpensive abundance has allowed energy consumption to be virtually ignored by many corporate organizations, including higher education institutions. The bills are now coming due for this neglect, and only aggressive and decisive action by university and college administrators will move higher education to a leadership position in energy and environmental issues. Added to the pressing financial demands of energy issues, the overwhelming environmental consequences of campus energy use are coming under the scrutiny of the academic community, not only to address issues of personal concern to members of the institutional community but also to incorporate the campuses into environmental curricula as ready-made laboratory exercises. These problems of energy use and environmental impacts are all compounded by the uncertainty of the energy future. Where will our electricity come from in twenty years? And at what price and effect on the environment? How will our buildings be heated and cooled? Can we afford to pay the energy costs of that new building so generously donated by well-intentioned benefactors? In this chapter, I describe the evolution of the energy management program at the University of Rochester, in Rochester, New York, as well as programs at other institutions. In particular, I outline the basic principles of energy management that apply to all institutions, large and small, and the role of students in the implementation of programs based on those principles.

Fundamentals of Energy Management

The key to success in energy management is to realize that it is, first and foremost, a business and therefore must have a comprehensive business

NEW DIRECTIONS FOR HIGHER EDUCATION, no. 77, Spring 1992 © Jossey-Bass Publishers

plan. Although a frightening thought to someone who has never formulated a good business plan, it is very simple to prepare *after* the homework is done, and quite impossible beforehand. I can personally attest to the fear and dread faced in writing a business plan for the first time (since I had never even seen a business plan prior to my first effort), but a quick trip to a management library for how-to guides (there are even software packages available now) should be sufficient.

Although I came to the University of Rochester to work on a doctorate in history, the facilities director, William Daigneau, did not hesitate to employ my engineering skills to reduce his energy costs. After complaining for several months about the lack of a coherent energy program, I was hired (on a part-time basis) as the university energy manager, largely on my assurance that, at the very least, I would save the university in energy costs several times the amount of my salary. I took several months to evaluate existing energy usage and to develop a business plan that outlined a five-year program involving more than $33 million in capital improvements. The first section stated the program goal: to reduce energy expenditures as much as possible within technical and economic limits without adversely affecting the mission of the university. The second section summarized the recommendations for remedial action and assessed the financial and environmental impacts, especially the cost of doing nothing, which is perhaps the most important cost to emphasize in the entire plan. At Rochester, for instance, current annual spending levels ($8 million for electricity, $2.5 million for coal and oil, and $6 million in central plant fixed costs) will amount to $330 million over twenty years without any inflation or growth factored in. An investment of $33 million in energy modifications will save over $60 million over twenty years, reducing the $330 million to "only" $270 million, with a net gain of $27 million after capital costs. (The cost of money affects all of these calculations, but the final result is quite similar.) The third section included a background of prior energy management efforts and their results, if any; a consumption management plan; a supply management plan; and an education and community awareness plan. Finally, the fourth section focused on the tasks of financing and implementing the recommended plan. I condensed the program outline into twelve pages of text, added an appendix full of numbers, turned it in on October 3, 1990, and by mid-November I was presenting it to the Board of Trustees, who formally adopted it. The five-year plan is updated late each summer and has grown to the current program that includes over $80 million in capital expenditures.

The keys to success with this program include keeping the goal in sight and following the rule of simplicity, for however complex the innumerable details, three rules guide the entire program: (1) If not needed, turn it off. (2) When on, make it operate as efficiently as possible. And (3) select the proper fuels and conversion processes for the particular situation.

For an institution that adopts a plan of this kind, the administration needs to assign specific responsibility for the energy management program in order to facilitate the implementation of these three rules. Almost always this task will be assigned to the facilities or physical plant organization. But wherever the specific responsibility is directed, it must also remain a clear responsibility of the administration as a whole.

Sources of Information: Energy Programs at Other Institutions

The best sources for energy management ideas are successful programs at other institutions. Energy management requires expertise in many different areas, including finance, marketing, economics, engineering, law, public policy, and history. The enthusiasm and intelligence of students can also be invaluable to the development of a viable program. Specific sources of good energy and environmental ideas are numerous, so I mention only a few that are sufficient to get started on formulation of a program. Walter Simpson (1990), energy officer at the State University of New York at Buffalo, wrote *Recipe for an Effective Campus Energy Conservation Program*, which is an excellent guide for use in developing a campus energy program. The Association of Physical Plant Administrators published *Energy Management* (Glazner, 1990) as one of the volumes in their Critical Issues in Facility Management series. More general sources on energy are available from the Association of Energy Engineers, the Illuminating Engineering Society, the American Society of Heating, Refrigerating, and Air Conditioning Engineers, and other professional organizations. Many campus programs have been featured in such publications as *American School and University* and *Facilities Management*. In particular, "Energy Management Tips" (1990), Orton (1991), and Simpson (1991) warrant attention. The *Chronicle of Higher Education* also includes articles about campus energy use, such as Collison's (1991) analysis of increases in electrical use in dormitory rooms as students bring in all the comforts of home, including stereos, televisions, videocassette recorders, microwaves, and computers.

Contact should also be made with other local institutions to share ideas that have worked in one's own community. Several energy users in Rochester formed an Energy Benchmarking Committee that meets once a month to share ideas and visit other plant facilities in the area. The marketing department of the local utility company (Rochester Gas and Electric) also works very closely with area institutions in the implementation of energy conservation programs and in the use of available rebate programs to pay for some (or even all) of the costs of certain energy conservation projects. The University of Rochester is the largest user of energy rebates in Rochester, receiving $180,000 to date with an additional $1 million expected in 1992.

Overview of Energy Management at the University of Rochester

The University of Rochester is a private institution with a current enrollment of forty-eight hundred undergraduates and twenty-eight hundred graduate students. More than seventy-five hundred full-time and twenty-four hundred part-time employees work in seven and one-half million square feet of facilities, including the 720-bed Strong Memorial Hospital and the Schools of Medicine, Dentistry, and Nursing, an academic campus with extensive research capabilities, the Eastman School of Music, and the Memorial Art Gallery. Over six million square feet are located at the university's River Campus along the Genesee River, served largely by a coal-fired central heating and cooling plant, with an annual consumption of forty-five thousand tons of coal and 120 million kilowatt-hours of electricity (an amount of electricity adequate to provide all electrical lighting in Great Britain in 1887).

Since the first oil crisis in 1973, attention to energy use and expenditures has drifted into and out of institutional consciousness several times, finally resulting in the establishment in 1989 of an Energy Management Office as a separate organization within the University Facilities Department. As energy manager, I head this unit, which includes a mechanical engineer, an electrical engineer, and an energy management system subunit that consists of a supervisor, a programmer, an automation mechanic, and five system operators providing twenty-four-hour coverage. Actual building operation and maintenance is performed by operation and maintenance groups on each campus, who are also responsible for energy budgets and expenditures in their buildings.

The Energy Management Office is primarily responsible for implementing the university's five-year energy management business plan, consisting of several capital projects and ongoing maintenance and operation of the energy management program. With total annual campus energy expenditures approaching $18 million, an organization of this size (with an annual budget of $500,000) was deemed appropriate for the University of Rochester. But each institution has to evaluate the functions to be performed and its own particular circumstances. Computer-based control systems, for instance, are available that can operate unattended, automatically calling designated individuals with detailed alarm messages. In other cases, the campus security office may be able to monitor the energy management system during off-hours.

Consumption Management

An institutional energy management organization and program, however elaborate and impressive, exists to reduce the impact of energy costs on institutional program delivery. This task involves application of the three energy rules, listed earlier, to everything on the campus that uses energy. The first of these rules, to turn off electrical devices when they are not needed, is perhaps the simplest in theory. The light switch, for instance, is one of the most fundamental tools of an energy management program and has the advantage of already existing in most spaces. In an office or other location where a particular individual is the sole occupant, a simple request to turn the lights off is usually effective. Occasional off-hour inspections and courteous reminders hung on the door knobs of offenders usually bring almost total compliance. Classrooms, hallways, lounges, and restrooms, however, are much more challenging. In these spaces, the use of automatic occupancy or motion detectors is almost becoming mandatory. (In fact, in New York State such detectors are now mandatory in new construction and renovations.) The two basic detector technologies are ultrasonic and infrared, and the two installation types are wall-mounted light-switch replacements and ceiling-mounted, typically with a separate transformer and relay. The many different manufacturers and options make selection difficult, but experienced users can usually offer recommendations. At Rochester, we tested some thirty different types of detectors from more than a dozen manufacturers before choosing six types from three manufacturers. Most electric utilities have rebate programs that pay some or even all of the cost of these detectors.

Outside lighting also needs to be controlled to keep it on at night and off during the day. Some institutions are evaluating programs to turn off certain exterior lights over holiday breaks or after certain hours, but any actions of this kind require careful consideration of potential risks and benefits. Photocells and mechanical time clocks are commonly used to control outside lights, but we have achieved excellent results by directly connecting the lights to the central energy management system and using sunset and sunrise times for on-off control. Daylighting is also used in some buildings, permitting the artificial lights to be turned down or off when adequate natural light is available. These applications require intensive analysis of the lighting system and controls, but they can result in significant returns.

Another major energy consumer that must be controlled is heating, ventilation, and air conditioning (HVAC) equipment. While, again, simple in theory, HVAC control can get very complicated. At one extreme is an administration building that is only occupied from 8:00 A.M. to 5:00 P.M. on work days. Here, a simple time switch can do the job, with some means for keeping the internal temperature above a minimum level. A basic time switch, however, is not aware of holidays or daylight saving time and requires at least two visits a year to make adjustments. The time switch is also unaware of the budget officer working on Saturday afternoon in coat and gloves and trying to read the energy management budget through frozen breath. Of the several solutions available to solve these problems, we use our energy management system to control all HVAC systems. Originally, this system turned systems on and off based on time of day and temperature, with weekly schedule adjustments for auditoriums and other facilities with variable schedules. A new control strategy is now being implemented that monitors the on-off status of lights as an additional input that determines HVAC operation. Since lights are on only when someone is present, that information can be used to activate the HVAC system for a particular space. If a room is empty, the individual room terminal box or fan coil turns off and the temperature is allowed to rise or fall to unoccupied limits. When the lights are turned on, the HVAC responds automatically to return the space to occupied conditions. If the room is served by a larger system, that system will be turned on if any of its served spaces is occupied and turned off when all are empty. This control strategy is being implemented in all campus buildings, fully automating the occupied-unoccupied decision-making process and eliminating the onerous ongoing task of changing the time schedules. In addition, the energy management system monitors actual hours of use and reports abnormal conditions, such as the lights in an office being left on overnight. This monitoring allows problems to be addressed immediately and identifies locations where occupancy detectors may be required.

The second consumption management rule is to ensure that energy is used in the most efficient manner. Adherence to this rule is usually not as straightforward as simply turning something off, but recent technological improvements have addressed many of the problems of energy efficiency. The most compelling area is certainly lighting. At Rochester, roughly 50 percent of our electrical consumption is used for lighting, with perhaps 10 percent of the campus cooling load required to remove the heat generated by these lights. One of the first projects undertaken by Patricia Beaumont as our newly hired electrical engineer was a quick once-over of the campus to identify incandescent bulbs that could be replaced with new compact fluorescents, and fluorescent fixtures that could be fitted with current-limiting bulbs. Nearly three thousand 60- to 150-watt incandescent bulbs, including seven hundred in the student center, were replaced with 5- to 18-watt compact fluorescents. In almost every instance, the amount of light was increased, sometimes dramatically. In addition, the new bulbs have an average life of ten thousand hours, compared to less than one thousand hours for the replaced bulbs, greatly reducing future maintenance costs. Special current-limiting bulbs were installed in many corridors, stairwells, and restrooms to reduce light levels that were above the recommended limits. These bulbs were entirely paid for by utility company rebates and produced a payback on the labor expended in six to eight weeks. At the same time, an extensive audit of all university lighting was begun by students employed by the energy office. After training, six student auditors were sent out to identify, classify, and quantify every luminaire and to record the information in a spreadsheet program. Beaumont then selected typical systems and modeled various lighting system modifications. The results clearly demonstrated that a combination of electronic ballasts and 34-watt T-12 bulbs and a combination of lamp removals and added reflectors produced the best return on investment. This information was then used with the remaining building audits to generate an estimate of $8 million to renovate more than sixty thousand light fixtures on the campus over a three-year period, cutting lighting energy costs by more than half. This program was included in the five-year energy management business plan approved by the university administration and is currently being implemented. Buildings already completed under this program have confirmed the savings projections used in the plan. In one building, Harkness Hall, over one thousand fluorescent bulbs were permanently removed, with increases in the available light in almost every space, except a few rooms that were grossly overlit before the renovation. Outside lighting is also modified where necessary, with high-pressure sodium bulbs replacing the older mercury fixtures and giving 5 percent more light at one-third the energy consumption. We are also evaluating polarized lenses for use in certain applications.

A simultaneous effort by our mechanical engineer, David Weed, targeted HVAC systems, which consume about 25 percent of campus electricity. After a thorough survey of existing building systems, the recommendation was made to convert most to variable volume operation and to replace existing pneumatic controls with computerized, direct digital controls. In simple terms, this conversion involves adding a variable speed drive onto a fan motor to permit the speed and air flow to be controlled on the basis of the load. Variable volume terminal boxes are added to each zone of the fan system and new controls are installed. These controls interface with the lighting status monitor system mentioned above, enabling the variable volume box to supply air to a space when it is occupied and to close off air flow when unoccupied. Since energy versus air flow is a cubic relationship, the energy savings are substantial. These controls also permit setpoints, air flow, and other parameters to be monitored and changed remotely, largely eliminating the need for a mechanic to respond to most hot and cold calls. Similar modifications were identified for laboratory fume hood systems, allowing air flow to be regulated based on fume hood sash position. Implementation of these changes in research areas has also permitted several other environmental safety concerns to be alleviated, particularly in regard to reentrainment of toxic fumes into building ventilating systems. The total cost for these modifications to nearly four thousand terminal units served by 350 fans was estimated at $5 million; the projects also were approved and are presently under construction.

Both the lighting and the HVAC renovations are undertaken in a complete energy renovation project for each building, reducing transaction costs and occupant disruption. After construction is complete, responsibility shifts to Daniel Scalia, supervisor of the energy management system, to write and install the software programs and to monitor ongoing operation efficiency, including daily monitoring of building energy consumption from meters connected to the system. We hope to refine the system software to the point where energy use can be predicted hourly based on time and temperature, with immediate reporting where consumption is outside the predicted range.

The third consumption management rule, selecting the proper fuels and conversion processes for the particular situation, is mostly concerned with the central power plant, but part of consumption management is to identify proper energy media use in buildings. Based on recommended supply management programs, hot and chilled water were selected for thermal supply use in all campus buildings at Rochester. A few heat pump systems, stand-alone refrigeration units, and electrical heat elements had been installed in various locations on campus, and these, along with building steam systems, will be replaced or modified to use hot and chilled water.

Supply Management

Unlike consumption management, which can describe situations and solutions that apply to virtually every institution, supply management can vary enormously from campus to campus and even between parts of the same campus. The identification and solution of supply management problems usually requires mo e specialized expertise than do consumption management problems. Various supply possibilities range from institutions that lease space with energy included in the rent, to urban institutions that have the luxury of purchasing economical chilled water and hot water or steam directly in usable form from a district heating and cooling system, and to institutions that generate all of their own heat and power. Most institutions purchase electricity from a local utility, and few things are so wildly variant across the country as electricity rates. In general, discounts for using large quantities are becoming rare, but discounts for using higher voltages are becoming more popular. In our own case, an audit of our electricity bills revealed that we could save $200,000 annually by abandoning our remaining 4,160-volt service. This involved installation of two transformers to convert 11,500 volts to 4,160 volts and resulted in a two-year payback. We are also looking at installation of a 115,000-volt substation that will save an additional $700,000 annually, also with a two-year payback. Also, it is essential at any institution that someone track down every electricity bill and verify that each bill is for a meter that actually serves campus buildings. I am continually amazed at the number of utility bills—especially electricity bills—that get paid for decades with no idea of what they are for.

Unless an institution is "blessed" with all-electric buildings, the other large energy expense is for heating fuel. Again, excluding those institutions in leased space or served by district heating systems, this fuel expense almost always pertains to natural gas, oil, coal, or some combination thereof. At Rochester, we primarily use coal, which has the advantage of being the same price now as it was ten years ago, effectively deflating our heating fuel cost by nearly 50 percent. The bad news is that coal is dirty and expensive to convert into a usable form of heat, such as steam or hot water. Our coal-fired steam plant was originally built in the mid-1920s, with a major expansion in the mid-1960s increasing boiler capacity severalfold and adding a fifteen-thousand-ton central chilled water plant with steam-turbine-driven centrifugal chillers. A historically unfortunate decision was made at the time of expansion to install large new boilers with the same steam pressure and temperature as those installed in the 1920s, completely ignoring the efficiencies to be gained from high-pressure designs. Coal and electricity were cheap in the late 1960s, and the designer, if cross-examined, would undoubtedly claim a defense of following "established engineering practices." More ominously, a report on university utilities prepared two years ago by a highly qualified engineering firm recommends the replacement of existing boilers with identical units when their service life expires in fifteen years. While recommendations of this kind may follow "established engineering practices," the university has ended up with a plant that requires twice the amount of coal to make a ton of chilled water that an efficiently designed facility would require, making it difficult to claim any sort of leadership position on energy and environmental issues. Having learned our history, we are now determined not to repeat it.

Ownership of a coal-fired power plant in an urban setting is a mixed blessing. Low cost and availability are certainly positive features, but drawbacks such as high fixed costs and detrimental environmental effects such as acid rain, ash disposal, and groundwater contamination from coal pile runoff continue to make coal a difficult fuel choice. We have a large oil tank at the power plant, but costs restrict this fuel to standby and backup use. Natural gas is available, but in limited quantities due to pipeline constraints that may or may not be removed in the near future.

After an intensive study of central power plant opportunities, including the possibilities of having a third party operate the plant or of abandoning it entirely and installing individual heating and cooling units in each building, several recommendations were made to maximize the economic return of the existing plant during the remaining fifteen-year boiler life. This plan has one long-term and three short-term elements. The first short-term element involves implementation of cogeneration by installation of a six-megawatt backpressure turbine to capture the available energy between the 175-pound boiler header and the 80-pound steam distribution system. At the same time, the existing steam-driven chillers will be replaced with new low-pressure absorption chillers. These new chillers also have the environmental benefit of eliminating several thousands of pounds of ozone-depleting chlorofluorocarbons. The existing steam distribution system also will be replaced over a period of years with a new low-temperature, hot water district heating system. These modifications will permit the university to generate approximately one-third of its annual electricity requirements without burning any additional fuel. The new chillers and district heating system will also reduce maintenance costs and provide more controllable environmental conditions in buildings.

The second short-term element is the installation of natural-gas-fired combustion turbine at the power plant. This turbine, a modified DC-10 engine, will generate all of the remaining campus power needs and, by capturing the exhaust heat, more than two-thirds of campus steam requirements. We are currently negotiating with our local utility to turn this turbine off during nights and weekends when they have excess power anyway and perhaps to sell excess power to them at other times when they need it. With this turbine, clean natural gas can supply much of our energy requirements without incurring additional operating costs, since natural gas costs more than twice as much as coal on a per-unit basis.

The third short-term element is the installation of a large steam turbine generator unit and the use of existing boiler capacity to generate up to twenty-five megawatts of coal-fired peaking power for the local utility for up to two thousand hours annually. This element is being evaluated almost purely as a financial investment for the university since it offers an attractive return on the investment required.

The fourth element addresses the long-term energy requirements of the university and involves construction of a new, clean, coal- and wood-fired power plant at a remote site, with hot water piped two miles to the existing central plant site. This new plant will be designed to have the least possible environmental impact on the local community. A potential fuel source is wood from a short-rotation forest that would permit the university to control indefinitely its energy future. A detailed study of this possibility is currently underway.

Student Involvement in Energy Management

Although it is possible to implement a comprehensive energy management program at a college or university without involving or even informing students, their involvement can be of great and mutual benefit. To cite my own case, as a doctoral candidate in history I am writing my dissertation on the history of the idea of cogeneration and district heating. I have had the advantage of employing other students to perform lighting audits, and I currently employ twelve students as energy management system operators, construction inspectors, environmental auditors, and general laborers. The installation of compact fluorescent bulbs throughout the campus was also largely done by students. They have also helped to move equipment between buildings and to dispose of old ballasts, bulbs, and fixtures removed during renovations. The involvement of students received a boost when one of my dissertation advisers became a dean and asked me to put together a course on energy and environmental issues. The result was an upper-level undergraduate and graduate class called the Politics of Energy and the Environment. Now in its fourth semester, this class has attracted students with a diverse range of talents and interests. The course begins with a history of energy and environmental concerns and progresses from a global perspective down to national, state, and local problems, ending with the campus and surrounding community. Each student prepares a course project in which he or she identifies an energy or environmental problem on campus, studies it in detail, and proposes politically acceptable solutions. Senior administrators attend the final class presentations and are encouraged to point out the merits or demerits of a student's proposal and presentation.

Topics studied thus far include conversion of university vehicles to natural gas, recycling, medical waste disposal, cooling tower siting, submetering of residence hall room electricity, installation of individual room temperature controls in residence halls, food waste, student desk lamps, power factor correction, and hydroelectric power for the campus. The natural gas vehicle study was very well prepared and has resulted in a test program involving two maintenance vehicles that use a natural gas compressor donated by our local gas company. The cooling tower siting study essentially narrowed the possible choices down to a single site; the work was comprehensive enough (including extensive input from faculty, staff, and students) that the site identified in the report was selected for the new cooling tower, which is now under design. Electrical submetering and individual room temperature controls received wide support from students and are currently being evaluated for an upcoming residence hall renovation. Two additional projects have demonstrated sufficient merit to be expanded into year-long projects for the students involved. The first of these is a report on the viability of using wood as a boiler fuel. Christine Poulos, an environmental studies major, argues persuasively that the university could utilize a short-rotation forest as a permanent fuel supply with great economic and environmental advantages. The possibility of controlling future expenses in this manner has received much interest from the administration, and Poulos is currently developing this concept as a senior honors project. The second is a study on the possibility of expanding the university's new hot water district heating system to serve other institutions and buildings near the campus. This report by Richard Mitchell, a public policy graduate student, has also generated interest within and outside the university as the problems that this system solves for us are by no means unique to higher education. Mitchell also discovered a program in the New York State Energy Office to encourage (and fund) such systems. Expansion of the district heating system would position the university in a strong energy and environmental leadership role in the local community and serve as a positive example for others in similar situations.

This list does not exhaust all of the student projects and opportunities at the University of Rochester. Other students are planning a prototype photovoltaic installation on campus, the use of electric vehicles by on-campus maintenance staff, and a campuswide refrigerator replacement program. Some Navy midshipmen in the Reserve Officers' Training Corp proposed a project to use the power plant as part of their engineering program, and the project is currently being conducted. Our plant modifications will include installation of naval ship instrumentation to assist in this effort. Overall, I have been very pleased with the involvement of students in both the planning and implementation of energy programs and intend to extend these programs as much as possible. Faculty and students are becoming more involved in energy and environmental issues in the local community, with the first effort being a conference on available energy technologies held jointly with the local Center for Environmental Information. The university has also been receptive to working these programs into the curriculum wherever possible.

Conclusion

The University of Rochester implemented a number of energy conservation programs since the 1973 oil crisis, but their effectiveness was never clearly demonstrated. At the very least, these programs lacked a clear objective and overall management responsibility. The current plan has corrected these deficiencies and has developed a coherent program to reduce energy consumption by more than half over the next five years without noticeable effect on university program delivery. Electricity consumption on the main campus, for instance, rose steadily from 24 million kilowatt-hours in 1961 to 114 million in 1988, while costs jumped from $320,000 to $7.4 million. In the past four years, we have not only stopped energy growth but also reduced overall consumption despite the addition of two new buildings and more intensive program use in existing facilities, resulting in an annual avoidance of $1.5 million in electricity costs. Our current major effort to renovate lighting and control systems will reduce electricity use by more than a third while improving occupant lighting and temperature levels. At the same time, cogeneration will produce much of our electricity requirements at a very low cost.

Even with these financial gains, the greatest enhancement to the program has been the inclusion of the academic and environmental community into the energy management process. Although still in an embryonic stage at Rochester, the potential exists at every institution for incorporation of students into campus energy and environmental programs. Whatever fields students choose after graduation, an intensive exposure to the realities of energy and environmental issues will make them not only better educated but also better citizens of the global community.

References

Collison, Michele N.-K. "As Students Cram Rooms with Electronic Gadgetry, Colleges Scramble to Meet the Demand for Power." *Chronicle of Higher Education,* Sept. 25, 1991, p. A1.

"Energy Management Tips." *American School and University,* August 1990, pp. 18–24.

Glazner, Steve. *Energy Management.* Critical Issues in Facilities Management, no. 6. Alexandria, Va.: Association of Physical Plant Administrators of Universities and Colleges, 1990.

Orton, Richard. "Retrofit Offers Solutions to Deferred Maintenance." *American School and University,* Aug. 1991, pp. 28–29.

Simpson, Walter. *Recipe for an Effective Campus Energy Conservation Program.* Cambridge, Mass.: Union of Concerned Scientists, 1990.

Simpson, Walter. "Conservation Produces Results." *American School and University,* Aug. 1991, p. 28b.

MORRIS A. PIERCE *is a doctoral candidate in history at the University of Rochester in Rochester, New York, and the university's energy manager.*

Colleges and universities can reduce their adverse impact on the environment, enrich the educations that they provide to students, and significantly reduce their costs of operation. Why is it so difficult to persuade them to do so?

Can Brown Be Green?
Lessons from One University's Quest
for Environmental Responsibility

James Corless, Harold Ward

The 640 students attending Brown University in the late 1800s appear not to have been a very healthy group. In addition to frequent gastric disorders, there were occasional outbreaks of typhoid, leading the university president to urge students toward more "sanitary" behavior. The cause of this distress turned out to be an outhouse behind the main dormitory, situated thirty yards from the well that served as the main source of drinking water for the school.

A century later, the six thousand students and two thousand faculty and staff at Brown University use two hundred and fifty million gallons of water annually, taken from the Scituate Reservoir located twenty miles to the west of Providence, Rhode Island. After use, most of this water is discharged to the Providence sewers and, after treatment, released into Narragansett Bay.

This dramatic increase in the scale and type of consumption shows that the Brown University of today is vastly different from the small cluster of ivy-covered buildings that sat on the hill above downtown Providence a century ago. The population has increased tenfold, the facilities have expanded to cover more than four million square feet in 233 buildings, including scientific research laboratories, libraries, office buildings, parking garages, and athletic stadiums. The resources needed to keep these operations running are substantial and expensive; each year we use more than 55 million kilowatt-hours of electricity, 23,000 barrels of heating oil, and 204 million cubic feet of natural gas, costing us more than $6 million.

NEW DIRECTIONS FOR HIGHER EDUCATION, no. 77, Spring 1992 ©Jossey-Bass Publishers

45

Clearly, the environmental impact of the university is no longer confined to our own backyard.

More Recent Observations

Issues of resource consumption on campus have been a focus of student class projects initiated by the Brown University Center for Environmental Studies (CES) since its opening in 1978. It soon became apparent that even when students were aware of the environmental consequences of their actions, there was often little they could do to reduce those impacts (for an exception, see Case Study 1 in the Appendix). Dormitory heating systems were old and unmanageable, thermostats were nonexistent or locked, light switches were key-locked or inaccessible, and many locations lacked adequate space for recycling containers.

The construction of a new university dormitory, the Thayer Street Quad, in spring 1990, appeared to provide an opportunity to remove these barriers to environmental efficiency. We hoped at the time that the university could avoid structural limitations of uncontrollable lighting and heating systems and provide space for recycling before the final floor plans were fully laid out. But the physical plant managers were apparently not prepared to accept outside ideas or even undertake basic research on purchasing efficient fixtures (and, even worse, were prone to downgrade efficiency to correct for budget overruns during construction). We sought to correct this deficiency by appointing an individual whose sole task was to research opportunities for minimizing energy consumption, increasing rates of recycling, and, in general, reducing the adverse environmental impact of everyday university operations.

In summer 1990, the position of environmental coordinator was created (and filled by one of the present authors, James Corless, several months later) in the university's Department of Plant Operations to identify resource conservation opportunities. Immediately, a proposal was developed to replace all of the incandescent fixtures in the plans of the new dormitory with compact fluorescents. Although suggestions to incorporate increased wall and window insulation and a dishwater hookup (to avoid using disposable products) in the lower-level snack bar were too late to be incorporated into the project, the lighting changes alone effected a $6,000 reduction in annual operating costs.

Initial attempts to set clear responsibilities for the coordinator's job underscored the importance of establishing priorities and agreeing on goals. Should efforts be focused on technical changes or community education? Were the results from a restructuring of the recycling program going to have a more beneficial effect than energy saved from retrofitting lighting in large office buildings? After several of the coordinator's cost-saving proposals stalled for months on end, it became clear that if Brown University was truly to commit to reducing its environmental impact, there needed to be a much stronger sense of importance and urgency applied to the effort. And, preferably, this priority should be endorsed at the upper levels of the university administration.

The "Brown Is Green" Initiative

The university administration was receptive to the idea of an initiative whose environmental goals would also yield economic benefits (see Case Study 2 in the Appendix), and, in January 1991, President Vartan Gregorian pledged that Brown would commit itself to a program of environmental responsibility with the colorful and optimistic name Brown Is Green (BIG). A BIG committee was appointed, chaired by Provost Frank Rothman, to investigate the potential for minimizing both resource consumption and the associated economic and environmental costs of day-to-day campus activities. The committee began by proposing principles on which the university could base its operating programs in order to increase resource efficiency and minimize economic and environmental impact.

The first BIG principle states that the university should, within limits of capital availability, invest in any resource conservation project that has an expected return on investment greater than the current borrowing rate. Not only does this principle make a significant step by phrasing the cost of a resource conservation project in terms of an investment (the rate of return on investment in energy efficiency often is much higher and more certain than are the rates of return from investments in stocks and bonds), it also suggests a mechanism to finance the project (assuming that the university is credit-worthy). The money paid back annually on a loan is compared with the money saved annually in reduced utility costs. If the latter is the greater of the two, then the project should be financed.

This BIG principle has not been easy to institute, probably because it requires a fundamental change in thinking. Even after acknowledging the validity of the principle in theory (that the cost of inaction is greater than the cost of action), administrators have recurring doubts about balancing a highly visible annual debt payment with utility savings that are hidden among much larger monthly bills. Plant managers regularly slip back into the mentality of treating energy efficiency expenditures as costs that compete with other plant operation expenses for funds in a limited budget, rather than as investments with excellent and secure rates of return.

At CES, we had better success with a student project that focused on four student dormitories scheduled to be renovated during summer 1991. By intervening early in the design process, we were able to incorporate energy-efficient lighting in all of the renovations. And by encouraging students to survey other students in the dormitories prior to the renovations, we were able to incorporate a lighting design scheme that provided both adequate room illumination levels and light quality acceptable to students. Through installation of fluorescent fixtures where incandescents would otherwise have gone, the project reduced future annual electricity costs by at least $16,000. The fixtures also qualified for rebates from the local power company, covering the incremental cost of the fluorescents and totaling over $100,000.

Another BIG project was initiated in summer 1991, with a paid student intern who investigated energy consumption in campus buildings. Brown's five science laboratories are by far the most intensive users of electrical energy, consuming over 40 percent of the campus total while accounting for only 5 percent of the gross square footage. A survey of building occupants and laboratory managers revealed that laboratory areas were significantly overlit and that occupants tended to leave lights on unnecessarily. (Occupants also tended to leave lights on even when they were not there—to give the impression that research never stops!) Laboratory fume hoods were also identified as sources of significant energy-saving potential. As many as 10 of the 127 fume hoods in the building were unused in any given year. Decommissioning of these unused hoods could have saved at least $10,000 annually ($1,000 per hood) by reducing heating and cooling costs.

Additional BIG principles are currently the focus of several student class projects. They include an analysis of appliance purchases in terms of total operating costs rather than initial equipment expenditure, an analysis of the additional cost associated with the installation and use of a dishwasher in the new dormitory's snack bar versus avoided purchasing and waste disposal costs, and a determination of the return on investment for replacement of many of the university's antiquated independent heating systems with high-efficiency alternatives. In Table 5.1, the BIG principles for a minimal economic and environmental impact are summarized and contrasted with the standard operating principles (the seemingly redundant Brown Is Brown) that we seek to supercede.

Lessons Learned

While we believe that the establishment of environmentally sensitive policies (such as the BIG principles) is an important first step, we have found that implementation of the policies, even with support from the top and the attention of a full-time coordinator, still presents challenges and frustrations. Some of the lessons that we have learned during this implementation process are as follows.

Make Every Effort to Work with (Not Independently of or Against) Offices or Individuals with Responsibility for Managing Campus Resource Consumption. Our experience has been that a new program or policy can often have significant territorial implications. Many schools have individuals within the physical plant who are involved in utility man-

Table 5.1. From Brown to Green: Present Versus Proposed Practices

Brown Is Brown	*Brown Is Green*
Invest only in resource-conserving projects whose financial savings will pay off the initial cost of the project within one or two years.	Invest in any measure to conserve resources that has a rate of return on the investment that beats the current borrowing rate.
Build or renovate buildings for the lowest initial cost.	Build or renovate buildings for the lowest life-cycle cost.
Purchase materials that are either nondurable or disposable. Purchase equipment with lowest initial cost.	Purchase materials that are either nondisposable or recyclable. Purchase equipment with lowest life-cycle cost.
Communicate with paper.	Communicate electronically.
Centralize billing for all utility costs. Spread costs evenly among university departments.	Hold individuals and/or each department accountable for consumption of resources. Reward resource-efficient behavior.

agement and who may already have responsibility for conservation projects, though their efforts may not be highly visible. For example, energy conservation efforts at Brown prior to BIG focused primarily on changes in mechanical rooms and basements, which building occupants rarely saw. Any outside person or new program must be marketed in terms of the ability to supplement, not supplant, ongoing efforts (with, perhaps, the promise of additional publicity), without implying that the existing efforts are ineffective.

Obtain Accurate Consumption Data and Compile Historical Billing Information. In order to evaluate the success of any conservation program, it is essential to have quantitative baseline data on consumption, cost, and even attitudes before the program is initiated. For example, in our most recent solid waste contract, we require that our hauler measure all waste and recyclables removed from the campus so that we only pay for what we throw away (we had been billed a flat fee under the previous contract). Without our most recent measurements, we now estimate that we are currently disposing of 30 percent less waste than what was paid for under the old contract. This should save us $40,000 in avoided tipping fees by the end of 1992. Henceforth, when we are asked how our recycling program is working, we will be able to respond in terms of tonnages and percentages rather than rely on qualitative assessments.

Stress Community Involvement, Educational Feedback, and Individual Accountability. Brown's utility bills are paid from a central budget and costs are not known by the occupants of individual buildings who control resource consumption. In some cases, this arrangement results in a uniform utility cost charged to all departments based on a general square-footage formula. Thus, those who conserve usually subsidize those who are more wasteful. Rarely are individuals or departments billed for the energy or water that they use, and hardly ever do they pay for trash by the amount that they discard. This uniform billing leads to a lack of accountability regarding consumption and generally promotes a carelessness among staff and students. A typical technical fix for this problem is to attempt to remove control from occupants (for example, by locking thermostats). We believe that increased accountability, through education and incentives (see Case Study 3 in the Appendix), is likely to be more successful than are measures such as isolating building controls from occupants.

We begin our educational efforts with basic information: the size of the annual campus energy bill, the cost of heating and lighting individual buildings, and the amount of solid waste that is discarded each month. This information is brought to the community through newspaper articles and presentations to students, staff, and departmental chairpersons. The BIG intern in the science laboratories found that occupants would be much more willing to turn off lights and machines if they could see the difference made by conservation. An engineering student currently is designing a visible energy meter (with a large, lit display reading instant demand and total usage from day-to-day), to be placed in the entrance of the building. We plan eventually to offer financial incentives for a department or dormitory to reduce its consumption by turning off unnecessary lights and turning down thermostats.

Use Pilot Tests to Support Arguments for Change and to Avoid Embarrassing Errors. With recent trends in environmental marketing, there is no scarcity of products that claim to be environmentally benign. We have learned to be skeptical consumers when purchasing products advertised as water-saving and energy-efficient. Several years ago, we allowed an energy-savings company to replace 75-watt incandescent bulbs in one of our dormitories with 7-watt compact fluorescents. The resulting dramatic decrease in light levels left a hundred students and several physical plant managers with a very poor opinion of compact fluorescents and of lighting efficiency programs in general.

Now, we ask first if a product has been used by other institutions with successful results, and if so, we then try it in a small-scale test location that can tolerate a failure. If the results are positive, they provide a stronger argument for a larger-scale project than if the product had merely been chosen from a catalog. On the other hand, if the pilot test fails, the result is much easier to accept on a small scale. This approach is not foolproof, however; we learned that even a successful pilot test cannot guarantee long-term success (see Case Study 4 in the Appendix).

Select Projects with an Educational Payback. A strong selling point for an education-based initiative such as BIG is the tremendous potential for students to study, survey, and count things that either the physical plant does not have time for or whose cost just to study exceeds any expected savings. Student projects have been a valuable part of our efforts to date. It was students who surveyed other dormitory residents about the quality of their showers with water-saving fixtures. The models that were identified as acceptable are now the only brands used by the university. It was also students who developed an acceptable, energy-efficient, dormitory room lighting scheme that was eventually adopted by the architects during the dormitory renovation projects. And it was students who inventoried showerheads, sink fixtures, and exit signs, allowing us to know exactly the right kinds of replacements to purchase and how long it might take, given labor costs, to complete a campuswide retrofit. These kinds of projects provide excellent educational opportunities for students in environmental studies courses, allowing the integration of specific hands-on tasks with the broader problem-solving contexts developed in the classroom.

Establish Program Priorities Based on Decisions That Are Pending. Our first success with BIG was the substitution of compact fluorescent bulbs for incandescents in the new Thayer Street Quad dormitories, with a projected annual savings of $6,000 and a rebate from the utility company of $26,000. Since lights were to be installed anyway, we only had to influence the *type* of fixture to be purchased, rather than to initiate an entirely new project. Had we been able to effect the purchase of windows with an energy-saving "low-e" coating in the new dormitory, the additional cost would have paid for itself in a couple of years. Now, the cost of an entire window replacement cannot be justified in terms of energy savings alone.

We have learned not to attempt to change everything at once. It is easy to underestimate the time needed to implement an idea. Selection of a few projects with attractive environmental benefits and cost savings, preferably those that can be achieved within the existing infrastructure, ensures a higher probability of success.

Use Savings from the Most Economically Attractive Programs to Fund Other Programs of Environmental Significance. On most campuses, there are a number of environmentally beneficial project possibilities with significant cost savings. Start with an examination of exit signs, where the financial savings can be substantial and the energy savings can be predicted with confidence since the signs are always lit (the only variable is the wattage). After such "low hanging fruit" have been plucked, remaining projects may offer lower or less certain returns and yet be highly desirable from an environmental perspective. We suggest that the profitability of a high-yield program be spread out over all programs; otherwise, the savings may be applied to general budget relief, and overly cautious managers may stop after the easiest and most lucrative projects are complete. Our initial attempts to apply this kind of thinking at Brown, however, indicate that it is easier to suggest than to implement.

A Plea for Networking

We urge everyone to share their ideas, their successes, and their failures. If we discover a type of recycled paper that fails in certain copiers or a faucet aerator that barely lets water flow, we want others to be informed about those products. Similarly, successful innovations at one institution can save time both in testing and in persuasion of plant managers at other locations.

In this chapter, we have tried to document the kinds of information and experiences that provide a means to those ends. Yet, to receive this information in minutes rather than months, we invite you to subscribe to an electronic mailing list created in February 1992 that is dedicated to sharing ideas and experiences from similar campus environmental initiatives nationwide. Under the name 'GRNSCH-L' (Green Schools), the mailing list is accessible through either Internet or BITNET and can be subscribed to by sending electronic mail to LISTSERV at Brown University.

Appendix: Case Studies from Brown University's Brown Is Green Program

Case Study 1: Taking Control of Our Actions—West House

In 1985, fourteen students moved into West House, a typical New England wood-frame house, and enrolled in a course on energy conservation. As part of a class sponsored by CES, students read meters, plotted consumption over time, and identified inefficient resource use. Thermostat covers were removed to allow resident control, the electric clothes dryer was abandoned, and weatherization materials were brought in. Since the program began in 1985, house residents have reduced energy consumption by 40 percent from the previous occupants' usage, primarily by more responsible building management (see Figure 5.1). Through an agreement with the physical plant, half of the total savings since the program began, over $3,000, has been set aside in a fund to pay for additional weatherization materials, compact fluorescent light bulbs, low-flow showerheads, and toilet dams.

Case Study 2: Exit Signs—Paying for the Costs of Inaction

In 1987, students from West House inventoried all of the exit signs on campus as part of their final project for an environmental studies class (the same class that teaches energy conservation techniques; see Case Study 1). Their proposal to change all of the incandescent bulbs to fluorescents was presented in detail to the physical plant the following semester. The $60,000 project investment, had it been made four years earlier, would

Figure 5.1. West House Energy Consumption, 1983-1991

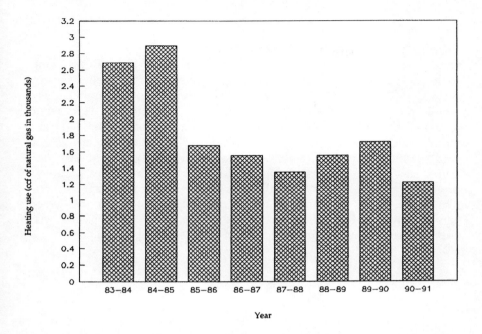

Note: Consumption figures have been normalized for an average winter; ccf = one hundred cubic feet.

have avoided energy and maintenance expenditures of almost $300,000. Only after the intervention of the BIG committee in mid-1991 did plant operations begin the changeover process. In a recent budget meeting, the university's vice president for finance mentioned this project as a bright spot in an otherwise dismal financial picture.

Case Study 3: Changing Habits Through Feedback and Incentives

In 1990, students in an environmental studies class conducted an experiment in six university-owned, off-campus houses (no more than seven to ten residents each) where students did not pay their own utilities. They mailed energy conservation tips and bimonthly charts of energy consumption to building occupants, comparing them to baseline figures from previous occupants. Occupants succeeded in reducing overall consumption by 10 percent, and, as promised at the beginning of the experiment, half of the savings ($1,000) were donated to a low-income weatherization assistance fund in Providence. When surveyed at the end of the program, the residents agreed that the feedback was a crucial factor in their efforts to conserve.

Case Study 4: No One Said It Would Be Easy!

Over three hundred tons of copy paper are used each year at Brown. One of the most highly visible opportunities for reducing environmental impact seemed to be a shift to use of a recycled brand. Knowing how choosy people can be about their paper, the university's purchasing department requested that we test any new paper in all major departments. After six months of extensive testing, one type of paper finally met everyone's requirements. We placed a large order with the company, only to find after four weeks of using it on campus that several copy machines began to produce spotted copies. Why hadn't this occurred during testing? Without notice, the paper mill changed the manufacturing process of the paper between the time that we tested it and the time that we purchased it. We are currently undergoing a second round of tests of recycled paper.

JAMES CORLESS is program coordinator for Brown Is Green at Brown University, Providence, Rhode Island.

HAROLD WARD is professor of chemistry and environmental studies and directs the Center for Environmental Studies at Brown University.

Changes aimed at reducing the environmental impact of the university can be most easily implemented using financial and institutional motivations.

The Environmental Ombudsman at the University of Kansas

Steven P. Hamburg, Susan I. Ask

Over the past decade many colleges and universities have grappled with how to effectively address environmental concerns. Contrary to popular belief, existing university administrative structures are successfully able to make changes. The difficulties in implementing change have less to do with the university than with the inherent nature of environmental concerns. In addressing most issues, the university tends to divide them into small, manageable units that do not necessarily pertain to the university as a whole. Environmental issues, however, are made up of an aggregate of factors that affect the whole university. In dealing with environmental issues, therefore, it is critical that problems and proposed solutions be considered on a universitywide basis. Unfortunately, the conflict between the tendency to divide problems into small subunits and the necessity to look at the larger picture has led to unnecessary and unintentional adverse environmental impacts in some institutions.

The University of Kansas, in Lawrence, has acknowledged the importance of addressing environmental issues as a whole institution while recognizing the need to work within operational units and their constraints. In developing the environmental program at the University of Kansas, the designers never seriously considered the establishment of an environmental bureaucracy and thus saved considerable time and money. Instead, the executive vice chancellor created the position of environmental ombudsman, with full powers of persuasion but none of implementation, and it has worked. While this office is less than two years old, it has already led to major environmental changes and, more important for the future, has had a positive institutional impact.

NEW DIRECTIONS FOR HIGHER EDUCATION, no. 77, Spring 1992 © Jossey-Bass Publishers

55

The Environmental Ombudsman's Office has been involved in a diverse range of projects, including formulation of an ozone depletion policy, increased recycled fiber content of the toilet paper purchased for the campus, solvent recycling, increased energy efficiency of lighting, and development of a campuswide program for recycling all paper. The cost of running this office is more than covered by the savings (avoided costs) attributable to the projects that have been undertaken. As the university community becomes more familiar with our efforts, the projects become easier to implement and more people bring new ideas to our attention. In this chapter, we describe the conceptual framework in which the Environmental Ombudsman's Office arose, some of the history that led to its formation, operational information about the office, and examples of projects that have been undertaken to date.

Working Within the Institution

In establishing a program to bring about positive environmental change, there are several key operational guidelines: (1) Change invoked for the sake of the environment cannot interfere with the fundamental missions of the university or its subunits, although it may alter how those missions are achieved. (2) Environmental change should not add a financial burden to the university as a whole. Consideration of the institution as a single unit is an important component of this premise. And (3) the impact of any change should be considered within the context of the entire institution as well as within the largest environmental context possible. For example, the effect of chlorofluorocarbons (CFCs) on the ozone layer should be examined globally, and fuel efficiency should be examined in terms of carbon dioxide production and global warming. These guidelines do not require extreme measures, yet, if applied rigorously, they lead to sound environmental and university policy. The reasoning behind these guidelines is developed more fully in the following sections.

Environmental Change and the University's Missions. Why is it critical that all changes be made subordinate to the missions of the university or its subunits? The reasons are threefold: First, the goals of the institution need to be established independently of environmental concerns, because no matter what it does, the university will have an environmental impact. If the mission statement defining those goals is well crafted, there should be many avenues for achieving them. It is then a matter of selecting the most environmentally benign approach or approaches.

Second, the moment that an environmental objective takes priority over a fundamental university goal, the issue at stake becomes political. We feel strongly that there are many environmental impacts within the university setting that can be reduced or eliminated without having to question the political hegemony of the institution. Once the process is politicized, it divides those affected into camps, diverting the discussion away from fundamental environmental issues and thereby reducing the probability of achieving the desired environmental objectives.

Third, sometimes the goal of an operational unit needs to be changed to fit within a larger university goal in an environmentally benign way. For instance, a housekeeping staff may define its mission as removal of trash from buildings at a set interval of every two days. When a recycling program is implemented, custodians are usually expected to handle the materials. But they can do so only if the garbage is picked up less frequently in order to have the extra time needed to handle the recyclables. While this change may be perceived as relatively minor by those receiving the service, it is in central conflict with the mission of the housekeeping staff.

Environmental Change Must Be Without Net Costs. Sound environmental policy should cost the university little, if any, money. This guideline is based on two presuppositions: First, since resources have an associated cost, the fewer the resources used, the lower the cost and impact on the environment. Second, costs incurred by one unit may be more than offset by the savings to another unit. The university must be viewed as a whole when weighing fiscal considerations.

There are many instances when a long-term investment, with a payback of longer than one year, is necessary to effect change. An example is the replacement of compressors or motors with more efficient models. When appropriate, reduction of social costs should also be considered a part of the return on investment. Social costs include any type of impact that is not valued in the marketplace, such as reduced contamination of groundwater supplies or decreased carbon dioxide production that affects global warming. However, most universities are so resource wasteful that, initially, enormous improvements in their environmental records can be made without having to give much weight to social costs and their nonmonetary returns.

When good environmental policy also results in good fiscal policy, there is little room for objection or debate. There are so many fiscally sound projects that, initially, it is not necessary to address projects that require large subsidies, except where hazardous material is involved. Once environmental projects are perceived to need monetary subsidies, they are too easily subject to political pressures and can be considered expendable. The requirement that environmental projects not cost much, if any, money will need to be reexamined, however, once the environmental projects with high payoffs are underway and the margin of savings starts to decrease.

Environmental Change Must Be Systems Based. The third guideline focuses on the need to take a systems-level perspective on the environment, a perspective that considers all interactions of the component parts. Without a reasonably complete analysis of the potential impacts and consequences of a proposed action on the university community and beyond, it is impossible to know whether an action is positive or negative, that is, advised or ill-advised. It is critical that an action have positive direct and indirect impacts, because it will end up costing more than it gains if there are negative impacts, and it will certainly be costly in terms of political support.

An example of positive and negative impacts resulting from a particular action is the replacement of a chiller with a more energy-efficient model that is significantly louder and thus requires a noise suppression system. The shortsighted perspectives of the past, which confined an analysis of a situation to the immediate time and place, have led to many environmental problems. Pesticide use on many campuses falls into this category. A systems approach may make people uncomfortable because many factors outside of their experience and awareness will need to be evaluated. However, this type of an approach is crucial to the goal of effecting positive change.

Antecedents of the Environmental Ombudsman's Office

The Environmental Ombudsman's Office evolved out of project and seminar courses taught by one of the authors, Steven P. Hamburg, on resource conservation that focused on the University of Kansas. These courses have provided important learning opportunities to both the students and the professor.

The first project course involved an evaluation of lighting in the main library. The student who worked on this project developed a set of reasoned and fiscally prudent suggestions that were presented to the dean of the libraries. Although none of the student's suggestions was implemented, the dean did request a review of the lighting plans for the new science library, which was then in the design stage. In that review, the proposed lighting scheme was found to be inflexible and inefficient. After a revised set of lighting plans turned out to be even more resource demanding, user unfriendly, and costly than the original plan, the problem was turned over to the collective efforts of a resource conservation class. The class developed a simple manual switch system that allowed the lighting scheme to be customized by library staff, at a cost lower than the original proposal. Student research also revealed the benefits of utilizing electronic ballasts, which were 30 percent more energy efficient than the proposed ballasts. The student-developed plan was implemented; it uses about 40 percent less energy to operate than was projected in the original proposal and at a lower capital cost.

A central precept of all of the student projects and of those undertaken by the Environmental Ombudsman's Office is that the investigator does not need to be an expert on the topic under study. Rather, he or she needs to employ critical thinking, serve as an effective researcher, and ask penetrating questions of the experts.

In 1988, Hamburg and Executive Vice Chancellor Judith Ramaley (now president of Portland State University) met to discuss some of the ideas that Hamburg's students had proposed over the years for reducing the environmental impact of the university. At a subsequent meeting concerning campus waste disposal, he agreed to undertake a semester-long study of paper use within the university, with the end goal of elucidating potential methods of reducing the long-term production of solid waste.

With the assistance of a graduate student and six undergraduates, Hamburg traced the flow of paper into, through, and out of the university and then constructed an analogue model of the process to aid analysis. Each student was responsible for a small, independent part of the project, which was not only an excellent learning opportunity for the student but of great benefit to the project as well. A comprehensive review of paper use was conducted, revealing that the university's waste stream was 65 to 90 percent paper and that about half of the paper waste originated in the state-controlled procurement process. The final report outlined specific recommendations. For instance, adoption of a plan for reducing paper use in the library's notification system for overdue books would result in $10,000 in savings per year. Also, greater use of double-sided copying would reduce the amount of paper consumed by fifty tons, with additional reductions in handling, energy, and disposal costs.

It is important to note that a reduction in disposal costs (the landfill tipping fee was only $5 per ton at the time) was not the only motivation behind the wastepaper study. The primary motivation was to help offset future social and regulatory costs of garbage disposal.

Impressed with the wastepaper report, the executive vice chancellor proposed a plan in July 1990 for a comprehensive environmental office on campus in which a faculty member would organize and direct the projects and students would serve as assistants. The vice chancellor offered Hamburg the opportunity to head this office, and together they worked to organize it. The selection of a name for the office was critical because it had to be value-neutral yet capable of invoking a strong image. An ombudsman is someone who intercedes within the system on behalf of an individual. An *environmental ombudsman* intercedes on behalf of the environment. This term seemed to best capture the spirit of the vision and of the role. It has served the university well.

When the Environmental Ombudsman's Office was set up in August 1990, there were four important provisions. The office would have a two-year trial period. Savings attributable to projects undertaken by the office had to exceed the cost of operating the program. The environmental ombudsman would report directly to the executive vice chancellor, with support from a small advisory board. And during the first two years, the office would undertake at least six projects. Because bureaucracies are slow to react, two years would be allowed to build a track record of consequence. At present, savings from the projects are more than covering the cost of operating the office. The practice of reporting directly to the executive vice chancellor has been very helpful in opening doors and getting people to listen, although we try hard not to make people feel that we are coercing them to make suggested changes.

How the Environmental Ombudsman's Office Works

During the first fifteen months of operation, we have worked on over twenty issues and projects, nearly five of which have been fully implemented. The basic approach adopted by the office is to identify and initiate research projects through which environmental impacts can be minimized. About one-third of the projects are suggested by students, faculty, and staff outside of the office. Once a project is initiated, either a student or staff member from the office takes responsibility for outlining the issues and gathering all relevant information, including university statistics and basic library research from regulatory, industrial, and nonprofit sources. Usually, this process takes several months, during which time the person responsible presents the relevant issues for discussion at the weekly staff meetings.

Once an issue is sufficiently brought into focus, a proposed action or concept paper is drafted. This one-to-three page document concludes with policy or procedural implications and recommendations. Next, a dialogue begins with the units or departments involved in the issue, leading to evaluation and refinement of the document, and then, finally, implementation. It is critical to note that a proposed action or policy is not discussed in a public setting until all of the affected parties have agreed to participate. This process takes time, but it allows the responsible unit or individuals to become vested in the issue and to take credit for the change, ensuring a high success rate.

The Environmental Ombudsman's Office has evolved in staffing over its first fifteen months. Initially, a part-time graduate assistant coordinated the work of the office, but during the 1991–1992 academic year, Susan I. Ask, the co-author of this chapter, was hired as a full-time associate environmental ombudsman. A full-time staff person to facilitate meetings and to follow through on projects has become essential to the functioning of the office. The dialogue between the undergraduate staff and the ombudsman is key to the success of the office.

Recently, an additional person has been hired to coordinate environmental awareness campaigns on campus that are related to the office's projects. Education is a critical component of successful institutionalization of change, and we are trying very hard to ensure that before changes are implemented, the university community understands why they are needed.

Projects Undertaken

Some of the projects undertaken thus far have been relatively straightforward, such as replacement of incandescent lights with compact fluorescents. Other projects have been more complex and innovative, such as development of a campus policy on ozone-depleting compounds.

Although a simple procedure, the replacement of incandescent bulbs with compact fluorescents across campus was complicated by bureaucratic factors. University energy costs are covered by a separate appropriation from the state, and therefore energy savings cannot be reallocated to pay for energy conservation measures. As a result, increased efficiencies are not accruable to the budget of facilities operations, which has to bear the initially higher cost of capitalizing the purchase of the fluorescent bulbs. The Environmental Ombudsman's Office worked with the executive vice chancellor and facilities operations to locate the funds to make the initial bulb purchases. In the future, bulb costs will be lower than if the replacements had not been made, and energy costs will be reduced, with a net savings to the university and state of $15,000 to $20,000 per year.

Another project involved the replacement of dormitory showerheads with low-flow models. Initially suggested by a student and researched as part of a course project, this effort has been largely championed by students. The Environmental Ombudsman's Office helped in the preparation of the proposed action, and later in the follow-through with the affected university departments. When a similar change had been implemented previously, the showerheads were vandalized, so our project met with resistance in the early stages of planning. However, student initiative convinced the administrator responsible for housing policy that the savings attributable to low-flow showerheads (lower water use, lower energy demand, and lower capital costs yielding a savings of $35,000 to $50,000 per year) would not be offset by increased repair costs. So far, the change has not encountered any problems. However, key to this success has been a concerted effort by students to educate their peers about the advantages of using the low-flow showerheads.

For the project involving development of a university policy on ozone-depleting compounds, we first worked with facilities operations to purchase two machines capable of reclaiming different types of CFCs used on campus, and then we required their recycling whenever possible. At the same time, the university also implemented a policy that requires all equipment containing CFCs to be drained before the equipment is removed from campus. These reclamation policies have led to a 30 to 50 percent reduction in CFC release on campus, resulting in savings that paid for the CFC-recovery units in less than one year. To further reduce the use of ozone-depleting compounds, our office has spearheaded the formation of a task force with representatives from all campus units involved in the procurement, design, repair, and safety of equipment containing ozone-depleting compounds. This task force has compiled an inventory of all ozone-depleting compounds on campus and their uses. They also are exploring ways to eliminate these compounds wherever and whenever possible and are preparing for the introduction of substitutes. Our goal is to be well positioned to take full advantage of any new technology and at the same time maintain the smooth functioning of the university.

A related project involves the proposed recycling of paint solvents through distillation. In collaboration with the Environmental Health Safety Office at the university, we formed a working group representing all users of paint solvents, both academic and service. Everyone agreed about the need to recycle our campus-generated solvents, but the logistics of where to house the distillation unit are currently being worked out. By reducing hazardous waste disposal costs, which can be expected to rise rapidly, the project will more than pay for itself.

Another area currently under study is the use of soybean-based inks in university publications. Despite the hype, we have not found evidence that these inks are environmentally more benign than petroleum-based inks. One can easily envision scenarios where the inks could be either *more* or *less* harmful to the environment than petroleum-based inks, but until there is evidence on which to base our judgments, we do not encourage the university to use soybean-based inks to minimize environmental impacts. Often, changes are made out of concern for known problems, yet a switch to a totally unknown and unproven material may prove equally damaging in time. It is important that the changes recommended by the Environmental Ombudsman's Office be informed by sound, up-to-date research, which is essential to establishing sound policy and ensuring our objectivity in assessments and recommendations.

Conclusion

We believe that it is possible to reduce significantly the impacts that a university has on the environment by incorporating common-sense perspectives into the operational structure of the institution. By looking at the larger context, we can reduce or eliminate many environmental impacts, with the secondary benefit of saving money. By requiring projects to be revenue-neutral, we have been able to avoid politicization of the projects that we have undertaken in the Environmental Ombudsman's Office.

In the future, as more environmental projects are undertaken by a variety of operational units of the university, we hope that these units will incorporate the guidelines of the Environmental Ombudsman's Office into their decision-making processes. We have every reason to believe that the University of Kansas will greatly reduce its environmental impacts over the next decade, as the concerns and remedial structures already exist and we need only to continue in our present efforts and direction.

STEVEN P. HAMBURG is a Charles Bullard Fellow at Harvard University for the year 1991–1992 and associate professor of environmental studies and of systematics and ecology at the University of Kansas, Lawrence. He is also director of the Environmental Studies Program and environmental ombudsman at the University of Kansas.

SUSAN I. ASK is associate environmental ombudsman at the University of Kansas and a recent graduate of the Environmental Studies Program. As a student she participated in the university wastepaper project and worked in the Environmental Ombudsman's Office.

A university's involvement in the stewardship of its place on earth
may lead to a healthier environment, but, more important, it offers
extraordinary opportunities for student learning.

Campus Environmental Stewardship

David J. Eagan

An Indian effigy mound in the shape of a bird, high on a hill overlooking
Lake Mendota, is one of several ancient mounds preserved on the University of Wisconsin-Madison campus. Built an estimated 500 years ago
by ancestors of one of today's Wisconsin tribes, it symbolizes the deep
and lasting relationship between people and the land. It is a reminder of
the timeless need for stewardship of the place that, for now, is home to
the university.

The above remarks are the explanation that I wrote for the logo of the
Campus Environmental Stewardship Initiative at the University of Wisconsin, Madison (UW), the project featured in this chapter. Once, while visit-
ing the mound—the outline of which suggests a hawk, a falcon, or,
perhaps, a swallow—I was struck by how well it symbolized the idea of
campus stewardship. The mound represents a past time and way of living
when people were more connected to the land, and now it is protected by
the university, tangible evidence that preservation of something for its own
sake is still possible at UW.

By virtue of its legal status as titleholder, UW, like every college and
university, is the obligate steward of its place on earth, regardless of whether
it realizes the significance of that role. For better or worse, its institutional

The author expresses his appreciation to the professors and others who helped
develop and guide this initiative. Special thanks to Duane Hickling, assistant vice
chancellor for facilities planning and management; David Musolf, assistant director
of the Institute for Environmental Studies; and students Mehrdad Azemun and Neil
Michaud. Funding was provided by the Center for Biology Education, University of
Wisconsin, Madison.

decisions influence local air and water quality, soil fertility, the fates of indigenous animal and plant species, and even human health. As the other chapters in this volume testify, the consequences of campus activities extend far beyond the institution's borders. It is curious that in a place where inquiry is so highly prized, the environmental impact of the campus has gone virtually unquestioned. Until recently, its own contributions to local, regional, and global environmental problems have been largely ignored. Equally lamentable, this lack of self-study and self-improvement has been a missed opportunity for enriching student learning.

But despite past tendencies, campuses can change the objects of their attention; they can broaden their sphere of inquiry to include their own activities. A college or university can examine and redirect its relationship to the environment, especially its *local* environment where it has the greatest influence over what happens. It can develop an institutional "land ethic" and reorient its behavior accordingly. The idea of stewardship suggests at least one strategy by which this reorientation process can begin. It calls for students, faculty, staff, and administrators to work cooperatively and over time to study their own campus, to begin to take responsibility for their individual and collective choices, and to discover the personal, ecological, and social implications of becoming responsible stewards of the place that, at least temporarily, has become their home.

The emphasis of this chapter is not on the obvious possibilities for local environmental improvement but instead on how campus stewardship can be integrated into the curriculum where it can serve many of the educational goals of the university. The stewardship initiative at UW engages students, as part of their coursework and with close guidance of faculty, in a critical inquiry of their immediate surroundings. No longer just a setting where education happens, the campus becomes a field station for applied scientific study, a place where academic lessons can be grounded in reality. The campus also comes to be seen from a very different perspective: as a dynamic, living ecosystem in which humans are but one component. Students are asked to look around them, ask hard questions, voice their concerns, and make a personal contribution toward understanding and improving both the community and the land.

From the time that the project began in summer 1991, the Campus Environmental Stewardship Initiative at UW has been a team effort, involving over one hundred students, a dozen faculty, and a growing number of administrators and staff. At present, the range of outcomes of this pilot effort are not yet known, but the ideas behind the project and its potential as a model for other institutions have generated enough interest to warrant a chapter in this volume. What follows is an explanation of campus stewardship—the potency of the idea, the components and structure of the UW project, and its impact and future possibilities.

The Idea of Stewardship

The word *stewardship* is rarely heard in educational institutions, particularly as it relates to ecological responsibilities. In higher education, the term is sporadically used to refer to the husbandry of such things as human knowledge, foundation funds, computer systems, and sometimes even academe as a whole. Yet, a perspective on stewardship makes eminent sense in schools, colleges, and universities: places where we transmit what is important about our cultures and our world. It is an idea with powerful implications for what we value, how we live, and, notably, how we educate.

From an ecological perspective, stewardship implies as much a way of thinking as a way of acting toward the land. It means learning about and taking care of a place, whether a natural area or urban setting, but it calls for care that is in the best interest of the place, not of the caretaker. Although definitions of stewardship vary, the human element is central: In places where people and nature coexist, human effort is needed to safeguard the integrity of the land and its inhabitants.

Stewardship was a central theme of the environmental visionary and writer Aldo Leopold, though it was framed at the time in terms of land management. Leopold was a professor of wildlife management at UW from 1933 to 1948, a period when public ecological understanding seemed to be in as short a supply as it today. In an essay written fifty years ago, he explains how a university education actually contributes to this lack of understanding, a phenomenon still much in evidence: "All the sciences and arts are taught as if they were separate." In reality, he continues, "They are separate only in the classroom. Step out on the campus and they are immediately fused" (Flader and Callicott, 1991, p. 302).

In the same essay, Leopold advances what could be interpreted as a call for campus stewardship. He advocates the idea of "all-campus teaching" of the principles of wildlife ecology, not only for future professionals but for everyone as an integral part of their liberal education. A cornerstone of this teaching, he insists, should be participation in "local projects" that provide "vital local facts and questions." "The objective is to teach the student to see the land, to understand what he sees, and enjoy what he understands" (p. 302). Putting this philosophy into practice on the Madison campus, Leopold and his students monitored the population dynamics of pheasants in an area known as Picnic Point, and they studied marsh birds at a wetland now covered, ironically, by the Biotron, one of the world's most advanced indoor facilities for biological research.

Practical insight on how to apply the stewardship idea, both ecologically and politically, and how it might function on college campuses is found in the work of The Nature Conservancy, a national organization committed to the preservation of threatened natural systems. For each of its preserves, detailed plans for stewardship are developed that include biological inventories, habitat restoration, ongoing monitoring, and even use of the site for education. A central element in these plans is the recruitment of local volunteers to help watch over the site. The reasoning is that local residents who have a long association with an area tend to be its best stewards. They regard the preserve as a valued part of their community and are inclined to be deeply concerned for its well-being.

An essential condition for effective stewardship is the long-term commitment by informed individuals who develop a relationship and sense of belonging to a place. This kind of connection to the land *can* happen with students in their four to five years on campus, though the current structure of the curriculum discourages local, long-term academic experiences. It can certainly happen with faculty and staff whose relationships may span decades. Wendell Berry, who even more than Leopold stresses the need for local, individual action, suggests that the process of becoming stewards of a place may be something deeply important to our lives, an essential element of our humanity. "The care of the earth," he writes, "is our most ancient and most worthy and, after all, our most pleasing responsibility" (1977, p. 14). The stewardship idea, as applied to the campus, not only embodies this responsibility but holds an extraordinary opportunity for learning as well.

The University of Wisconsin-Madison Initiative

The Campus Environmental Stewardship Initiative, currently in its pilot phase, aims to develop a mechanism by which the core ideas of stewardship can be worked into both the operations and the curriculum of the UW campus. It is rooted in the belief that the process of paying attention to the university environment will have the greatest impact if it becomes an integral part of the educational mission of the institution. Seen another way, the initiative offers a means to connect what happens in the classroom with what is happening immediately outside. It aims for the kind of fusion of science and art that Leopold envisioned, with students engaged in a cooperative effort to raise and address local questions.

The first task in stewardship is to understand the ecological and organizational setting, in this case of the UW campus. Founded in near wilderness 140 years ago, the university has altered the essential character of the land more completely than any other factor or event in the 10,000 years since glaciers last covered the area. Its nine-hundred-acre central campus is an amalgam of buildings, roads, landscaped open spaces, and wooded natural areas that reflect land use decisions and institutional priorities that have evolved over the decades. In years past, to cite one example, extensive marshlands on the west end of campus were drained or filled in, initially to combat malaria around the turn of the century, and later to dispose of construction debris and power plant ash. The Class of 1918

Marsh, a fourteen-acre vestige of those wetlands, was restored to its former status in the 1960s after over 45 years as a cornfield (whose grain, by the way, fed Leopold's pheasants, which have since died out).

Today's campus has 330 buildings, over twelve miles of roads, and eleven thousand parking spaces. Its boundaries contain many acres of forest, four miles of lakeshore, a channeled stream, and a marsh. UW is the daily home of forty thousand students and sixteen thousand faculty and staff and is the residence of sixty-eight hundred students and eighty dairy cows. It is also home to a few white-tailed deer, a thriving population of raccoons, and an uncommon water lily. By its population alone, the university would rank as Wisconsin's eighth largest city, with an environmental impact to match.

Using this dynamic setting as a laboratory, students participating in the initiative undertook studies—as part of their coursework, and with faculty guidance—in two broad, often overlapping areas. Some students conducted research on traditional areas of campus environmental concern such as lake pollution, energy efficiency, pesticide use, and solid waste disposal. Other students investigated campus natural history, documenting the diversity of plants, amphibians, microorganisms, and other cohabitants and studying physical aspects such as geology, hydrology, and soils. The initiative is unique in having this twin emphasis. At other institutions, campus-focused environmental research rarely acknowledges the link between environmental issues and local campus ecology and neglects to tie the study of complex issues such as pesticide use with the basic biological and ecological dynamics of campus lawns and woodlots. From the perspective of stewardship, both areas of inquiry are necessary to reach a balanced environmental understanding.

Within their topic area, most of the student projects addressed the questions, "What's going on?" and "Who's in charge?" Using interviews, scientific fieldwork, and university records, students documented historical precedents and current operations, examining campus policies and decision-making procedures. In their project reports, to the extent possible, they also proposed recommendations for improvement. Their diverse and fascinating findings about the campus environment, along with notes on relevant organizational structures and suggestions for change, will be compiled into the *Campus Environmental Profile*. This document, to first appear in 1992, will present the kind of ongoing composite portrait of the university needed to guide informed stewardship decisions.

The student research projects and the profile were the main objectives of the initiative in its pilot year. Obviously, not a lot of what could be called active stewardship occurred over this period, at least not environmental action based on the work of the students. But since stewardship can only happen with the support of good baseline information, that data collection task is where we have put the initial emphasis. From an educational point of view, however, the benefits of stewardship activities, for the students as well as the organization, can begin right away. The initiative provides ways to get students involved, to give faculty a central role, to leverage the cooperation of administration and staff, to strengthen the academic mission, and to make visible headway in a very short time. Its design has a built-in flexibility that can accommodate an evolving level of commitment by an institution: It can involve a few professors or dozens, and it can focus narrowly or comprehensively on elements of the campus-environment relationship.

Initiative Design. Descriptions of the central features of the initiative's design and operation illustrate how it fits within the curricular and administrative structures at UW. These elements could transfer easily to most kinds of educational institutions.

Use of Existing Courses and Curricular Structures. The initiative utilized existing courses, specifically those requiring individual or group projects. In most classes that participated, faculty invited students to focus their projects on course-appropriate questions related to campus natural history or to environmental issues. Some projects incorporated both perspectives, such as the study that examined the impact of storm runoff into the lake, which required a calculation of campus rainwater flow rates as well as an assessment of off-shore species diversity. The number of students volunteering in these classes ranged from one to twenty.

In two courses, participation in campus-focused projects was required of all students. Within these two models (voluntary versus required participation), there are two general types of studies: one-of-a-kind projects devised by students that may or may not ever be repeated and longitudinal projects in which students collect data to update ongoing campus research.

In summer and fall 1991, five courses (one with a laboratory session) participated in the pilot, and a sixth, the certificate seminar, agreed to share its findings for inclusion in the *Campus Environmental Profile:*

1. Limnology—Conservation of Aquatic Resources/Laboratory: Zoology 315/316
2. Introduction to Entomology: Entomology 302
3. Design, Restoration, and Management of Native Plant Communities: Landscape Architecture 666
4. Principles of Environmental Science: Environmental Studies 126
5. Economics of Recycling: Agricultural Economics 575
6. Environmental Studies Certificate Seminar: Environmental Studies 600

Student projects varied widely within and across these courses. In Economics of Recycling, seven students divided into three different projects to examine the new university recycling system, recycled paper purchasing, and the refillable coffee mug program at the student union. Of the twenty participants in the limnology course, most examined biological aspects of Lake Mendota, including one team that landed two thousand young fish in a single sweep of their seine. In the entomology course, all forty-five students were asked to collect a minimum of fifteen different insects from the campus as part of their required collection of seventy-five insects. This assignment added over 650 new records to the insect inventory from Picnic Point and the Class of 1918 Marsh. And a group in the landscape architecture class developed management and land use plans for forested areas on campus.

The most intense investigation of the campus environment was conducted by students in the Environmental Studies Certificate Seminar, a capstone experience designed as an integrative analysis of a complex issue. For the first time ever, the seminar focused on the environmental impact of the UW campus. The forty-eight seniors in the course conducted detailed assessments on twelve topics, including pesticide use, electricity consumption, campus land use decision making, wastewater policies, and recycling. One of the consistent findings was the need for more and better campus record keeping. While most participating courses required students to present their findings in class, the capstone seminar hosted a more formal presentation in the union theater and invited campus staff, administrators, and the public.

Faculty Involvement. Because of the educational orientation of campus stewardship, faculty members play a central role. They provide academic and technical direction for the student projects and make the pedagogical linkages within and between disciplines. They also confer a degree of scientific credibility and respectability to the effort. The initiative involved faculty from five departments, all of whom signed on with the expectation that their participation would not significantly increase the time that they could devote to their respective courses.

Faculty also provide continuity to this initiative. Effective stewardship requires a long-term commitment to the tasks of acquiring data and monitoring change. Insect diversity and fish populations vary through time, as do annual purchases of chemicals and costs of waste disposal. Significantly, all five agreed to perpetuate the campus-focused studies as far into the future as possible. Despite the fact that initial support for coordination of the pilot effort was limited to ten months, each faculty participant felt strongly enough about the stewardship idea to continue the project, regardless of funding.

Administrative and Staff Support. This kind of environmental self-analysis requires the willing cooperation of those whose performance is under scrutiny. Even at a public institution in a state with liberal open-records laws, staff were more forthcoming with information and assistance when they saw their roles as partners in the stewardship process. With environmental issues becoming increasingly sensitive subjects on campus, it proved to be as important to cultivate good relationships as to generate good data.

There was broad support for the stewardship idea across the university, from top levels of administration to custodial staff, even when that support involved exposure of problems in need of significant attention. There was general agreement that this exposure was something that the campus could and should undertake, for practical as well as political reasons. And the link with undergraduate education proved essential. Because the student research was conducted as part of classwork, staff took information requests seriously and made themselves more accessible. They appreciated the fact that their time and effort would benefit numerous students through class presentations, and through the sharing of reports kept in the stewardship library. The long horizon and improvement orientation of the initiative were also important, contributing to the favorable impression that the student projects were part of an ongoing improvement process and not just designed to uncover dirty laundry.

As an extraordinary example of administrator accessibility, a group of students studying campus land use set up a meeting with the assistant director of landscape architecture and planning but found their allotted hour too short to cover all of the issues raised. The assistant director suggested that they come back the following week, and this invitation started what eventually became an informal seven-week seminar for the students. To provide the information that they needed, he invited a variety of campus experts each week to join the discussion. This was a unique case, but it shows the potential for engaging nonacademic personnel as valuable contributors to undergraduate education.

Central Coordination and Stewardship Library. Although the actual work of stewardship is carried out by students, faculty, and staff in their respective areas (and it is essential that responsibility for action remain with those closest to the issues), it was helpful to have someone coordinate the research projects, keep track of environmental activities and information, and develop a comprehensive understanding of the place. My role as project director included meeting with faculty, explaining the initiative to classes, working with students to help design their studies, cultivating administrative contacts, and providing resources such a campus maps and reports. It also involved development of an expanding collection of resources and UW-specific data, which became the core of the stewardship library.

With the able assistance of two undergraduates, I began the process of pulling together information related to campus biodiversity and environmental impact that was scattered in faculty files and archives and available in personal stories of informants throughout the university. In addition, we collected and organized the materials generated by the student projects, which included campus planning documents, annual reports, environmental impact statements, maps, photographs, interview notes, and the final project reports. This collection is now available to professors, students, and others as a resource for future campus studies and related research.

Campus Environmental Profile. Although still in the planning phase, the profile will be one of the most visible and compelling outcomes of the stewardship initiative. It will be a state-of-the-university-environment report covering the campus natural environment as well as traditional issues. Accordingly, it will serve as both a product and a process, reporting past and current findings of the campus inquiries as well as helping to inform and direct future efforts.

Written primarily for internal use, the profile will tell the unfolding story of the natural history of the UW campus, reporting species diversity, population changes, restoration efforts, and geophysical dimensions. It will chart the current status of environmental issues such as energy use, waste disposal, pesticide application, indoor air quality, and recycling. It will also alert readers to the magnitude of campus environmental concerns and provide recommendations for remedial actions. Its contents will come from many sources, reflecting the team effort involved in pulling the document together, and its areas of focus will accommodate the needs of the institution and the interests of its contributors. In a sense, the profile will be a public conversation about what is happening at the university, why the events are important, and what might be done to improve environmental policies and practices.

Outcomes and Future of Campus Stewardship

Even at this early stage, some of the outcomes of the stewardship initiative are apparent. Foremost are benefits for the students, who consistently report their appreciation for the chance to make a contribution, to see their course projects have at least potentially positive consequences for the campus. They also value the all-too-rare glimpse into the workings of the university and, especially, the contact with administrators, staff, and others who run the institution. Some of those who studied Muir's Woods, the marsh, and other natural areas of the campus expressed strong feelings toward those places and counted the time spent there as a highlight of their semester. And, to infer a benefit, the student research projects provided an important opportunity to learn and refine scientific process skills through practical, applied inquiry. Students discovered that this kind of research is not an abstract exercise but is, instead, closely interwoven with the politics, economics, and history of a real institution.

There were positive results for others as well. Faculty members saw the pedagogical value of having at least some students in class focus on the campus and share their results with others. They also recognized the scientific and practical value of having available a comprehensive collection of data about the campus environment. Nonacademic personnel were unexpected beneficiaries, with many wishing that they had more of these kinds of interactions with students. Several said that they recognized in their role in the institution at least some responsibility for educating students—a role that, regrettably, goes largely untapped.

The campus stewardship idea, especially over the long run, holds a number of potential benefits for the institution. Although it is too early to know where its greatest influence lies, it can contribute to the university's broad goal of improving undergraduate education, and, more specifically, of enhancing academic objectives such as science literacy and problem-solving and critical thinking skills. The *Campus Environmental Profile* and the stewardship library, which will funnel campus environmental data into a central location, are likely to be helpful resources for students, administrators, professors, and the public. Finally, in the tradition of the Wisconsin Idea (the notion that the borders of the campus are the borders of the state), the lessons of campus stewardship could lead to more responsible environmental citizenship and intelligent local action elsewhere, led by UW alumni who settle primarily in the state.

As for future developments in environmental stewardship at UW, there are many possibilities. A much broader range of courses could be involved, and student research could reflect a greater partnership with the administration through projects focusing on specific campus problems. Courses in history, sociology, education, and engineering, for example, could broaden the scope of the profile by furnishing information on social and technical dimensions of the campus environment. But participation in campus stewardship need not occur only through formal classes. Projects could be done for independent study credit, or as student organization activities. Several undergraduates even suggested personal long-term projects, which, started as freshmen, could span their years on campus. Especially at large universities such as UW, they said, it would be a way to cultivate meaningful relationships with faculty, staff, and the campus itself. Beyond student projects and research, the initiative might also broaden opportunities for learning through innovations such as a campus natural history laboratory and museum, an interpretive trail system, educational landscaping, environmental displays and exhibits, and behind-the-scenes tours of campus operations.

Rethinking What Education Is For

The stewardship initiative did not arise in isolation. It draws some of its ideas from efforts elsewhere and extracts some of its inspiration from the growing interest in and quickening pace of campus environmental change nationwide. In 1991, for example, Tufts University (see Creighton and Cortese, this volume) and the University of Georgia were the first to have their top executives endorse official policy statements calling for stewardship and for environmentally sound campus practices. There have been recent state-level conferences on campus pollution prevention in Washington, Minnesota, and Washington, D.C., and on campus recycling in California. Several publications have appeared on the "greening" of colleges and universities that cite dozens of campus activities (for example, Capone, 1991; Student Environmental Action Coalition, 1991; Cool It!, 1991; Integrated Solid Waste Management Office, 1991; Brough, 1992). The Environmental Protection Agency recently initiated a "green campus" award for two-year institutions (Stanley, 1991) and is considering a similar award for four-year schools. And, significantly, there are the beginnings of an epistemological debate that calls into question how colleges manage their environmental affairs and how they teach and conduct research (see Orr, 1990, 1991a, 1991b; Berry, 1989; Wilshire, 1990).

Beyond practical outcomes such as reduced energy bills and healthier air, campus environmentalism is starting to alter perceptions about what higher education is for, what is worth learning, and what graduates ought to understand and do about environmental concerns. It is these potential changes in the nature of education that hold the brightest hope for bringing about change in our behavior toward the environment. But for colleges and universities to realize this educational potential, they need to better recognize their essential role in fostering this kind of grounded learning.

Campuses are often regarded as microcosms of the larger society, or, worse, as somehow separate from the real world. Both conceptions are dangerous if they lead people to regard what happens on their campuses as irrelevant or insignificant. Quite to the contrary, universities are very real places with significant environmental impacts, on a scale with cities, towns, corporations, and major institutions. At UW, the impact of sixty thousand individuals and a billion-dollar annual budget is about as real world as one can get.

From the perspective of stewardship, colleges and universities are not distant abstractions but rather full-fledged analogues of the kind of social and economic organizations in which students will spend most of their lives and where environmental problems will be just as real as they were on campus. Like cities and corporations, colleges are political, bureaucratic, and hierarchical, and they tend to ignore persons who have little influence and power. They may, however, have a greater openness to the idea of self-evaluation and a greater wealth of skilled individuals and resources that can be brought to bear on problems. And, increasingly, they are places where the environmental status quo is called into question. Thus, a university campus may be the best place available to learn about stewardship, and to participate in what amounts to an apprenticeship for acquiring the skills needed for a lifetime of environmental inquiry and action.

Will the Indian mounds on the UW campus, more than a dozen in all, still be considered worthy of protection in another 140 years? And which of the comparatively recent monuments (the administration building, Badger Stadium, the new parking ramp) will become our legacy? Although it requires a stretch of the imagination, campus environmental stewardship offers students the opportunity to contribute to the construction of a new sort of monument—a sustainable campus—which would be visible evidence of their commitment to an idea and would retain the mark of their personal contribution. Students might someday come back to see the forest that they studied and helped restore, or to get an energy consumption update for a building that they helped renovate. If the stewardship idea works, they might also develop a lifelong sense of connection to the place that, for now, is home to the university.

References

Berry, Wendell. *The Unsettling of America: Culture and Agriculture.* San Francisco: Sierra Club Books, 1977.

Berry, Wendell. "The Futility of Global Thinking." *Harper's Magazine,* 1989, 279 (1672), 16–22.

Capone, Lisa. "Magna cum Environmentalist: The Environmental Imperative in Higher Education." *E Magazine,* 1991, 2 (2), 37–41.

Brough, Holly. "Environmental Studies: Is It Academic?" *Worldwatch,* 1992, 5 (1), 26–33.

Cool It! *Students Working for a Sustainable World: The Cool-It! Project Directory.* Washington, D.C.: National Wildlife Federation, 1991.

Flader, Susan L., and Callicott, J. Baird (eds.). *The River of the Mother of God, and Other Essays by Aldo Leopold.* Madison: University of Wisconsin Press, 1991.

Integrated Solid Waste Management Office. *Fifty-Three Simple Things Universities and Colleges Can Do to Reduce Waste: Case Studies of University Source Reduction, Recycling, and Composting.* Los Angeles: Integrated Solid Waste Management Office, Board of Public Works, 1991.

Orr, David W. "The Liberal Arts, the Campus, and the Biosphere." *Harvard Educational Review,* 1990, 60 (2), 205–216.

Orr, David W. "Rating Colleges." *Conservation Biology,* 1991a, 5 (2), 138–140.

Orr, David W. "What Is Education For?" *In Context,* 1991b, 27, 52–55.

Stanley, Ron. "Interview with Barbara Frank, Director, Pollution Prevention Education Committee." *Community, Technical, and Junior College Journal,* 1991, 62 (2), 6, 8.

Student Environmental Action Coalition. *The Student Environmental Action Guide.* Berkeley, Calif.: EarthWorks Press, 1991.

Wilshire, Bruce W. *The Moral Collapse of the University: Professionalism, Purity, and Alienation.* Albany: State University of New York Press, 1990.

DAVID J. EAGAN holds degrees in biology and anthropology and is a doctoral candidate in the higher education program at the University of Wisconsin, Madison. He is project director for the Campus Environmental Stewardship Initiative.

Before the Hendrix Local Food Project started, over 90 percent of the food served on campus came from outside the state. Today, 30 percent comes from Arkansas and there are plans to reach 50 percent in three years.

Hendrix College Local Food Project

Gary L. Valen

The Hendrix Local Food Project facilitates the purchase of food from local producers in order to improve the nutritional quality of cafeteria meals, stimulate community well-being, and promote environmental sensitivity on the campus of Hendrix College, in Conway, Arkansas. We use the project to teach students about the foods that they consume and to be a positive participant in the local economy. The desired outcome is a win-win situation that meets the needs of the campus population and earns respect and support from the people who live in the same region as the institution. As a demonstration of the principles of the multiplier effect, money spent in our local economy is turned over from two and one-half to five times in the community, which means more money for the college's neighbors. In addition, the college community collectively contributes to both a healthy environment and a sustainable future by easing the reliance on fossil fuels for food delivery and by stimulating the production of nutritious food in close proximity to the campus.

As a major purchaser, Hendrix College has been a force for change in the local community through its preference for products that are grown in an environmentally responsible way. Farmers have responded to the new market and compete with each other to meet the college's expectations. While it is a small beginning, the application of similar techniques on college campuses across the United States could spark a major revolution. If dining facilities in other institutions such as hospitals, corporations, or government agencies also became markets for local food producers who use healthy and environmentally sensitive production methods, the potential to make the agricultural infrastructure more sustainable is tremendous.

NEW DIRECTIONS FOR HIGHER EDUCATION, no. 77, Spring 1992 © Jossey-Bass Publishers

Traditional Campus Food Delivery Services

A college food service is one of the most discussed and least understood aspects of a modern campus. With food as the object of derision in the residence halls and even classrooms, cafeteria workers routinely endure comments about mystery meat and disappointing meals. The high traffic of pizza delivery trucks around residence halls at mealtimes suggests that students on some campuses are resorting to an expensive alternative to their meal plans. Schools typically require their residential students to eat in the college cafeteria as a way to ensure sufficient revenue to keep the operations in the black.

What is generally not known is that collegiate food operations are a big business. The annual budget for Hendrix College, with its one thousand students, is over $1.5 million, including summer conferences and outside catering. Usually billed as an auxiliary service, the meal delivery system on a contemporary campus often provides extra revenue that administrators can use to fund athletics, facilities, social events, or other special projects. Food vendors are often selected on the bases of low bids and sometimes special perks that are provided to senior administrators. In addition, food brokers often control menu items by aggressive sales promotions and special relationships between sales personnel and cafeteria management. It is rare to find nutritional quality of meals or sources of food consumed by student patrons even mentioned in the annual cafeteria contract negotiations.

There are notable exceptions, but the general attitude about campus food is disdain or, at best, tolerance by the students and a sympathetic acceptance of the status quo by the faculty and staff. Even in places where administrators make an effort to please their student diners, the quality of meals often gives way to fast food or shopping mall selection systems. The nutritional and environmental impact of the ways that food is grown and transported is usually not considered by cafeteria operators, college officials, or even the people who eat in the dining halls. If a campus community elects to become environmentally sensitive, the food service is a good place to start.

Origins of the Hendrix Project

The Hendrix Local Food Project emerged from a desire to implement a wellness program on the campus. The Office of Student Development, in association with certain key faculty members and with the blessings of the president, embarked on a year-long study of wellness during the 1985–1986 academic year. A committee of faculty, administrators, and students defined wellness at Hendrix as the promotion of student growth through physical fitness, good nutrition, psychological well-being, and global awareness. The global awareness component included a desire to become a more environmentally sensitive campus community, and improvements in nutrition required a change in the basic operation and philosophy of the college cafeteria operation. By the 1986-1987 academic year, projects were set in motion to enhance student opportunities for growth in each of the wellness areas.

The most difficult aspect of the wellness project was to find ways to improve student nutrition. Before 1986, our college food service followed the practices of most institutions in the United States by offering meals that were prepared mostly by the suppliers of the food products. Inexpensive transportation and the growth of a large food industry in the 1950s and 1960s replaced older meal preparation techniques that utilized local commodities and cooks. The advantages of the new system were ease of preparation in the college cafeteria and a wider variety of food choices. The disadvantages were that the quality of the meals, including the nutritional value, was no longer a prime concern and all commodities had to be trucked to the campus over long distances. As a result, students became less satisfied with their meals and the local farmers lost a major customer for their produce.

The first steps toward the Local Food Project were taken in 1986 when four Hendrix students spent the summer determining the origins of foods that were served in the college cafeteria. The study was directed by the staff of the Meadowcreek Project, an environmental education center in Fox, Arkansas, and supported by a $57,000 grant from the Jessie Smith Noyes Foundation. Meadowcreek served as a nonprofit consultant to the students and the Hendrix Office of Student Development.

The student researchers traveled the country with notepads and a video camera in search of the actual sources of commodities that were served in the cafeteria. When video and written reports were shared with the Hendrix community at the end of the summer, the results were shocking. Only 6 percent of the cafeteria food came from Arkansas, a state with a strong agricultural economy. While beef cattle grazed within sight of the campus, the meat served on campus came from a large feedlot operation in Texas. Since cattle raised under the stressful conditions of confinement in a feedlot do not have the same flavor as range-fed beef, fat from Iowa was added to the meat to improve the taste, and then the beef was shipped to the campus.

Vegetables and fruits came to Hendrix from California, over two thousand miles away. The growers in that state admitted to the students that their products were developed to survive the long truck ride, and there was little concern for the nutritional quality. Many vegetables were frozen, canned, or packed in chemical preservatives to maintain a long shelf life. Tomatoes were picked green and artificially ripened by a gas process. A special type of strawberry was developed with a high fiber content for a better appearance to potential customers. While these commodities looked appealing, their taste and nutritional quality were diminished.

As a consequence of this eye-opening research, students, faculty, and administrators expressed a strong desire for the cafeteria to obtain more food products from local farmers. Unfortunately, there were many obstacles to using fresh, area commodities for students meals. The food service had lost its capacity to prepare fresh foods. Preprepared meal products supplied by the industry could be heated and served without the services of qualified cooks. A return to the previous pattern of serving fresh foods would require the college to hire more skilled staff, resulting, in turn, in a significant increase in meal charges to the students. Since the students of a private college must pay their own costs or seek financial assistance, it was not practical to increase the board rate in a significant way even for better food.

A second problem was that local farmers had lost their ability to compete with the major companies in the production of vegetables, grains, dairy products, and meats. The agricultural land surrounding Hendrix was used to produce goods that were shipped in raw form to food handlers in distant cities. Farmers were not able to deliver their products to the cafeteria in a form that could be used by the meal preparers. Since the food service did not have a large storage capacity, local foods were available only at limited times during the year. Farmers were also not able to compete with the larger suppliers for the price of their products. The heavily subsidized food industries in major urban areas are able to charge less for their products because external costs such as transportation and labor are borne in part by the federal and state governments.

Even the student consumers in the dining hall presented problems for the use of locally produced goods. Many young people have been raised on the convenience foods of the 1970s and 1980s and would not be satisfied with the more basic, nutritionally sound foods that were common in the less complex world of earlier generations. In addition, the students have grown up in a society that can supply almost all types of produce throughout the year due to a sophisticated transportation system. These young consumers do not comprehend the seasonality of commodities that are grown in their own communities.

In spite of what appeared to be insurmountable obstacles, we were determined to move toward the utilization of local foods in the cafeteria. It made sense for the nutritional goals of the wellness project, the well-being of the student diners, and the strength of the local economy. Many area farmers and community leaders also expressed support for the project.

Implementation

The food project was set in motion during the 1988–1989 school year with the continued support of the Meadowcreek Project and a $157,000 grant from the Winthrop Rockefeller Foundation in Little Rock, Arkansas. The stated goals of the project were to find ways to increase the use of locally produced foods in the college cafeteria and to educate the students about the benefits of nutritious foods. Our desired outcomes were better health for both the students and the local economy.

Our first step was to hire a coordinator, a task that proved more difficult than expected. Since the food project was a new concept, there were few candidates who could meet all the requirements of the position. The present training programs for food service personnel emphasize the use of prepackaged meals, so no qualified individual was located in the traditional markets. Looking elsewhere, our search committee hired a woman with a master's degree in horticulture and a strong personal interest in nutrition as the project coordinator. She was also raised on a small farm and knew how to communicate with rural people. The selection of the right person to direct the project was a crucial step. It had to be someone who understood the fundamental philosophy of the project and was able to generate enthusiastic support from other people, who were likely to be skeptics. The job also required someone willing to be something of a revolutionary.

Before the project coordinator was hired, an administrative structure was established to support her position. The food project coordinator works directly for the director of the food service, and her office is located in the kitchen area of the cafeteria. She has daily contact with the food service staff and with people who eat in the cafeteria. She is available to help the cooks with menu preparation, to talk with suppliers, to educate the students about good nutrition, and to learn every aspect of the college's food operation. We also had the commitment of the director of the food service, who supported the project and accepted the coordinator as a participating member of his organization. He supplies specific and realistic technical information about food preparation techniques and large-scale menu planning.

As the vice president for student development, I provide oversight of the Local Food Project. I am the direct liaison with the Rockefeller Foundation and with college staff and administration. A project of this magnitude requires someone who can keep goals in focus at times when the food service staff becomes burdened with problems or small details. A committee made up of Hendrix faculty, administrators, and students also provides suggestions and helps to secure acceptance of the project goals among other members of the Conway community. The Office of Student Development and the Food Project Committee serve as promoters, while the coordinator and the food service staff implement the specific details of the project. This system provides both the practical and inspirational dimensions required to alter established procedures of food preparation and delivery.

Creating a Food Project

The remaining goal of this chapter is to provide suggestions to any institution that wants to use its food service as a means to become more environmentally sensitive. These recommendations are a direct result of my experiences at Hendrix during the first three years of the food project. While each college or university will have its own structures and challenges, the following outline is presented as a general guide.

The first problem that a new coordinator faces is to determine how to change a food system that has probably existed for years. Perhaps the biggest challenge is to enlist support of the cooks and servers. Even with the hard-won endorsement of the president, faculty, students, and administrators, the cooks and servers can make or break a food project. The Hendrix coordinator spent many hours helping with meal preparation, serving luncheons and banquets, learning the personal history of fellow workers, and becoming, simply, a trusted member of the team. It was only after several months of these activities that enough of a bond was established to begin a discussion about altering meal preparation techniques or, even more radical, changing recipes. This kind of rapport is crucial because it is not useful to bring in fresh local produce if the cooks refuse to prepare the food in a tasteful manner. Since the servers have daily contact with student diners, they are in the best position to promote good nutrition or encourage someone to risk a new menu item. The breakthrough became apparent at Hendrix one day when a long-time cook declared, "Oh, you want to fix meals like we used to."

A second suggestion is that support from the college community must be ongoing and consistent. The coordinator, along with the major proponents of the project, must continue to enlist support and conduct a continuing educational program on the campus. The dining hall patrons need to know why the menus are changing and will probably be supportive if they know that the changes are in response to environmental concerns. Campus meetings, the school media, residence hall lounge discussions, and faculty retreats all serve as places to promote a local food project. A newsletter and campus bulletin boards are other promotional opportunities. The support committee should meet on a regular basis and be given specific tasks, such as menu testing and promotion, and feedback opportunities. The Hendrix study became a source of community pride early in the project, which helped to maintain momentum through the difficult stages. There is good evidence that community pride also improved the attitude of students about the entire food service operation.

Third, there is an immediate and easy step that can bring desirable publicity and help jump start the project: Buy as many commodities as possible within the state where the institution is located. The food purchaser can easily direct all present suppliers to search their inventories for locally produced food. *Locally produced* can mean different things depending on the region. Hendrix defines the term as food grown and processed within about an hour's drive of the campus. If some foods are not available locally, sources within the state are sought. The 1986 student survey revealed that the rice served in the Hendrix cafeteria came from Mississippi. This was an astounding discovery because Arkansas is the largest rice-producing state in the nation and there are representatives of the rice producers on the Hendrix Board of Trustees. This situation was easily remedied with local rice suppliers. Commodity brokers will respond and even suggest sources if the college or university requests local and state food, although we found that we could not rely on them to fully endorse our search for suppliers.

The decision to buy within the state brought Hendrix favorable statewide attention. Meal items prepared with Arkansas produce are labeled with a small state emblem that informs the student diners about the source of their food. Menus are also prepared around special state products, and a few food producers rewarded the cafeteria with special promotions. This immediate step of in-state purchasing provides a strong start for and brings support to the more difficult aspects of a local food project.

A fourth step is the actual identification and patronage of local suppliers of commodities. This is a difficult process because in contemporary agriculture there are typically few local farmers who produce a goods that can be immediately transformed into meals. For example, right next to a campus, there may be a dairy farmer who must send milk to a distant city for processing and then have the products shipped back for sale. While there is no immediate solution to this situation, the food purchaser can at least seek dairy products from the closest processor. When a food service searches for local suppliers of meal items, it must take the long view that a demand will eventually stimulate suppliers. Among other advantages, use of local suppliers reduces the amount of fossil fuels that are expended in the delivery of food products.

Information requests to county extension agents and local farm organizations, and visits to the local farmers market, are excellent ways to identify local producers. The project coordinator at Hendrix located a number of serious gardeners who expanded their crop inventories to meet the college's needs. The coordinator and the county extension agent arranged workshops and seminars to help the producers prepare for a commercial market. Meetings of this kind attract potential suppliers and also provide a base for a produce cooperation venture.

A successful food project requires a spirit of cooperation between the cafeteria employees and the producers. The locations of farmers who can supply eggs and dairy products should not be difficult to determine in most states. These commodities are routinely delivered to markets in the local areas and are easy to find. Local suppliers of meat products may be more difficult to find due to the widespread use of confinement systems and processing centers that are scattered across broad regions and require extensive shipping. Our difficulty at Hendrix was partially solved when an organic beef producer received a U.S. Department of Agriculture permit and began a slaughtering operation on his farm. Poultry producers are difficult to find outside the major confinement producers. A veteran Hendrix cook suggested that we process our own chickens in the dirt-floored basement of the old cafeteria, as cooks did in the old days, but the suggestion was politely rejected.

One last consideration with local producers is the delivery structure. It is costly and inconvenient for food service employees to deal with the delivery of small amounts of produce at random times during the day. Our solution at Hendrix is to designate one farmer as a delivery person. All the producers agree to leave their commodities at one location, and a standard weekly delivery schedule is followed. Planning is underway to establish a food brokerage center, complete with chilling shed and other storage facilities. In most communities, this strategy may establish new businesses as institutions become more selective in their food-buying habits.

The project coordinator at Hendrix also helps by publishing a list of foods to be used each week in the cafeteria. This list is useful for both delivery and production planning. Every year an estimated food-purchasing list is distributed to area farmers. Spring and fall plantings reflect the anticipated demand so that costs are held down with the elimination of waste and overproduction.

A fifth area of consideration for a campus involves the question "How can changes in the cafeteria systems improve the environment?" The answer is both simple and complex. As the consumer, the institution can stipulate that it wants food products grown or raised in ways that are environmentally sensitive. This stipulation becomes complicated when one attempts to define the term *environmentally sensitive*. Should all produce be grown using organic methods? In most states, it would be difficult to obtain a full range of products from organic producers. On the other hand, if a school says that it will purchase organic commodities whenever possible, it may stimulate an increase in organic farms. A new chapter of the Ozark Organic Growers Association was established in the county where Hendrix is located as a result of the new market provided by the food project.

Organic produce is often expensive because it is scarce and has a strong market in select areas of major urban centers. Our food service at Hendrix found that organic producers sell products with slight cosmetic blemishes at greatly reduced prices for use in the salad bar or prepared dishes. If food purchasers become acquainted with producers, special arrangements can be made for price reductions.

As a market, the school should let its suppliers know that certain standards are expected. We require that food served in the Hendrix cafeteria be grown using sustainable agricultural methods that enrich the soil, use minimal energy, leave marginal land out of production, and result in humane treatment of animals. Our project coordinator is personally acquainted with the producers and regularly visits their farms. In addition, suppliers attend meetings on the campus and eat in the cafeteria. The personal relationship that exists between the college consumers and the producers has established a working relationship that permits an ongoing dialogue about environmental concerns related to the way that food is grown. We are able to achieve our environmental goals by maintaining a direct relationship with the producers that goes beyond the simple purchase of their commodities.

A sixth area of consideration is the educational component of a food project. The cafeteria is an excellent place to teach diners about the foods that they are eating. The coordinator at Hendrix attempted many complicated instructional methods, including table tents, posters, newsletters, and charts, before the adoption of a simple and effective system. Presently, each entree is labeled with a card that has a pie chart showing percentages of calories derived from fat, protein, and carbohydrates. The chart also gives the calorie count for each serving. In addition, the card has a heart sticker if the selection meets the guidelines of the American Heart Association and a state sticker if it is made with Arkansas products. Food items from local suppliers often include the name and location of the farmer. The analysis of the entree is made easier with the help of a nutrition software package that is designed to create special diets for medical facilities. We use Nutritionist III from N-Squared Computing in Silverton, Oregon. Most college or university computer centers have a list of nutritional analysis programs. The American Heart Association, National Dairy Council, American Cancer Society, and the American Institute for Cancer Research all provide excellent references for free or at minimal cost.

The coordinator at Hendrix publishes a newsletter for students and staff that features health information about meals as well as stories about the farmers who supply commodities and their efforts to minimize environmental impact. A nutritional library is available in the computer center for those who want more information. The coordinator also presents programs in residence halls on the food project and helps students learn about nutrition and environmental issues. The food project at Hendrix is now a regular part of the campus wellness program.

As a final suggestion, make sure the time frame for the food project is long enough for cafeteria personnel, farmers, and students to get used to the idea. Food service directors are naturally hesitant to change proven methods of doing business. Yet, most eventually see that the practice of purchasing local food is good for public relations. They also learn that serving more fresh foods and being identified with an environmental movement is advantageous as well.

Outcome of the Hendrix Food Project

When the three-year grant period is over at Hendrix in 1992, the food project will continue. Farmers now depend on the cafeteria market and have their own motivation to provide commodities. The food service personnel are trained to inform students about their meals, and a complete library of information cards, charts, and nutritional information has been established. We intend to seek additional funds to help local farmers continue their movement toward a cooperative organization or to set up some type of local food brokerage facility.

The project will continue because it has been successful. In contrast to the 6 percent ($45,000) level before the project began in 1986, over 30 percent ($212,000) of the food served in the Hendrix cafeteria now comes from within the state of Arkansas. That statistic will improve gradually because there is a commitment to continue buying in the state. New local businesses have been formed as a direct result of the study, and that increase will improve the rate of local purchases. The University of Central Arkansas and the Conway Regional Hospital have expressed interest in obtaining commodities from the farmers who serve Hendrix. Since the project has always been viewed as a long-term enterprise, there is a natural evolution and momentum that will keep this effort alive in the coming years.

To be sure, the food project at Hendrix did not end all of the complaints about cafeteria food. Institutional food is never as good as home-cooked meals, but that fact alone is not always the problem. Contemporary life-styles are such that more than half of the U.S. population's daily meals are eaten out of the home.

A college or university may be the first place that students are exposed to balanced meals. Dissatisfaction with institutional food often comes from their desire for "normal" food: hamburgers, pizza, or other fast food staples. Here it is important to recall the original intent of the food project. An educational institution has an obligation to teach students about all aspects of life, including proper nutrition and the environmental consequences of food production. Students are asked to develop new habits and to gain knowledge in the classroom; it seems reasonable to expect them to do the same in the cafeteria.

Future of the Food Project

Hendrix College will continue to promote and increase the use of locally produced foods and to improve the nutritional quality of its cafeteria meals. The experience of the food project has demonstrated the need for a nutritionist to join our cafeteria staff. In addition, our plan is to have students serve on a general food service committee that advises the managers about ways to improve the meals. A second student committee is being formed to continue the study of methods to make the food service more environmentally sensitive. This committee will work with the kitchen staff to recycle waste, locate additional sources of local produce, and promote the goals of the food project on the campus.

We shall seek additional grants to support local producers in the delivery of commodities to Hendrix and other area institutions. Hendrix is in the unique position of being a market in search of suppliers. Based on our experiences during the first three years of the project, we hope to increase the variety of produce that is available to the cafeteria. Since Arkansas has a limited growing season, it will be necessary to develop some type of food preservation and storage facility in the Conway region. We intend to raise our local food purchases from 30 percent to 50 percent within the next three years. This effort will require a major commitment from producers to find ways to extend their seasons and to experiment with food items that are not now grown in the area.

To respond to the growing number of inquiries about the Hendrix Local Food Project, we prepared a set of materials to help others develop similar projects. A six-minute videotape, a manual that provides a step-by-step guide, and a brief brochure are now distributed to college campuses, environmental agencies, and food producer organizations. It is our hope that the Hendrix project will be replicated at numerous college and university campuses, leading them toward greater environmental sensitivity in the coming years.

GARY L. VALEN is vice president of student development at Hendrix College, Conway, Arkansas. He also serves on the boards of Meadowcreek, an environmental education center in Fox, Arkansas, and the Kerr Center for Sustainable Agriculture in Poteau, Oklahoma. As the owner of a small farm, he has a strong interest in the promotion of sustainable agriculture and the revival of local communities.

This initiative, designed by students in a two-college town, encourages purchase of locally produced food as one means of developing a sustainable agricultural economy.

The Campus and the Biosphere Initiative at Carleton and Saint Olaf Colleges

Eugene B. Bakko, John C. Woodwell

Traveling through the fields of southern Minnesota, a summertime visitor is impressed with the expansiveness of agriculture. Save for trees in town and along river corridors, the land is used to grow food. Crops on rolling hills continue to the crest of the farthest hill, then to the crest beyond. What are these crops? Who grows them, and using what methods? Who consumes this food? Is this land being used in a sustainable manner?

Students of Carleton and Saint Olaf colleges, in Northfield, Minnesota, sought answers to these questions, and to the questions of how the two colleges participate in this agriculture and how they might participate more closely. What foods do the colleges feed their students? Where do these commodities come from? What are the downstream effects of their production? What are the local alternatives? Can redirection of the food purchases of two small colleges toward local producers help support the regional agricultural community?

The authors gratefully acknowledge the assistance of Karl Stauber of the Northwest Area Foundation; Ed Buchwald, the Carleton adviser to the Campus and the Biosphere initiative; Roger Nelson and Mark Wilson, directors of the Saint Olaf and Carleton food services, respectively; and the farmers, administrators, faculty, staff, and other friends who made the project possible.

For a copy of "Education in a Hotter Time: The Campus and the Biosphere in the Twenty-First Century," "Financing a Local Foods Project with Energy Savings," or the eleven-minute video "The Campus and the Biosphere," please contact Eugene Bakko.

With support from the Northwest Area Foundation, the help of a full-time manager, and an adviser from the faculty at each campus, five students from each college began the Campus and the Biosphere initiative in fall 1989. Students were chosen competitively from a pool of applicants and worked a self-scheduled average of ten hours per week throughout the school year. While all students received a stipend, some arranged to apply part of their experiences to for-credit independent studies.

Working with the directors of the two college food services, students waded through invoices, noting what the colleges buy and at what prices, and tracing the high-volume items back toward their respective points of origin. The students also surveyed local food production, researching its availability and diversity, with an eye toward finding locally grown alternatives to imported food. They probed the true costs of the colleges' food-purchasing habits, investigating the energy used in the food production and researching the problem of pesticides in water and food.

Recognizing that a plan to redirect the colleges' food purchases into more sustainable practices might cost the colleges money, two students worked full-time during summer 1990 looking for ways that the colleges could save money. They found one route in another environmentally friendly project: a plan to retrofit some of the colleges' older lighting hardware with new, energy-efficient equipment. In the context of the food project, the plan was to earmark part of the net financial savings to offset the higher prices of locally and sustainably produced food.

The primary objective of the Campus and the Biosphere program is redirection of the colleges' food purchases toward local agricultural products. Among local producers, we have taken a special interest in those who use *sustainable practices,* in the broadest sense of the term: agriculture that uses few or no chemicals and little nonrenewable energy, and that is part of a distribution system characterized by less intensive processing. Noting the success of the local food and economy initiative at Hendrix College, in Conway, Arkansas (Valen, this volume), we estimated that the combined food budgets of Carleton and Saint Olaf (in excess of $2.5 million) might be large enough to make a substantial market for local growers of fresh produce. We were hopeful that a food cooperative could keep supplies steady and reliable, as achieved at Hendrix. Further, we hoped that our efforts, successful or not, would contribute to the education of both academic communities.

The Colleges as Buyers

First came the appraisal. Using spreadsheets big enough to stall a personal computer, the students divided duties as they sought answers to the first set of questions: What do the colleges buy, in what quantities, and at what prices? Where is this food produced, and how?

The answers were hard-earned and incomplete. While the checking of quantities and prices was straightforward enough (a lengthy exercise in invoice review), the task of tracing food items back to their sources was an involved and complicated process. In all, the students spent three and a half months on this inventory and tracking effort, substantially more than we had originally anticipated. Most fascinating, and most frustrating to the students' efforts, was the degree of complexity in the distribution system, and the ignorance of each player about all the other players. The meat buyer for the colleges' primary food purveyor was unable to name even the state in which most of the beef was raised. Asked where they got a particular type of food, the wholesalers' nearly universal response was "from all over." With these sorts of answers, queries about pesticide use or other details yielded few useful results. We were left with the clear impression that within much of the industry, food comes from the person who answers the phone at 1-800-GET-FOOD, and that is the end of the story. Frustrating as it was, however, the experience was an eye-opener; it drove home to us the magnitude and intricacy of the machine that we were studying.

Even so, the students did determine that the two colleges, within a state that is a net exporter of food, import from outside Minnesota 81 percent of what they eat (Figure 9.1). California and Florida lettuce, cucumbers, broccoli, and fresh fruits make their way to the college, as do dry beans from South Carolina, pineapples from Hawaii, hamburgers from Pennsylvania, and apple juice, melons, and grapes from Argentina, all testimony to the immensity of the food distribution system.

With hard-earned details of the colleges' food purchases, the students set out to find appropriate candidates from whom to buy locally produced food. They ran abruptly into a major problem: the growing season in Northfield, Minnesota, is short and inconveniently timed (Figure 9.2). While fresh Minnesota-grown produce is available from late June to late October, most students are on campus for only two months of that time. For consumption in the fall or spring, season-extending technology is required, although there is a trade-off between reduced energy use in transportation and increased energy use for extended storage. Canning of fresh fruits and vegetables uses roughly four times as much energy as the transportation of fresh produce from California, with freezing taking six times as much (Figure 9.3). Six months of refrigeration, at half the energy consumption of transport from California, is an option, but only for produce that stores well, and students do not clamor for cabbage and brussel sprouts.

The students agreed that meat, dairy products, and select vegetables were the best candidates for redirection of purchases because they are available all year from local producers. In fact, 14 percent of the colleges' food budgets go toward fresh meat, with dairy products taking 16 percent. After a review of the alternatives, the students concluded that the colleges could raise in-state purchases to at least 39 percent of total food purchases

Figure 9.1. Current Sources of Some of the Colleges' Food

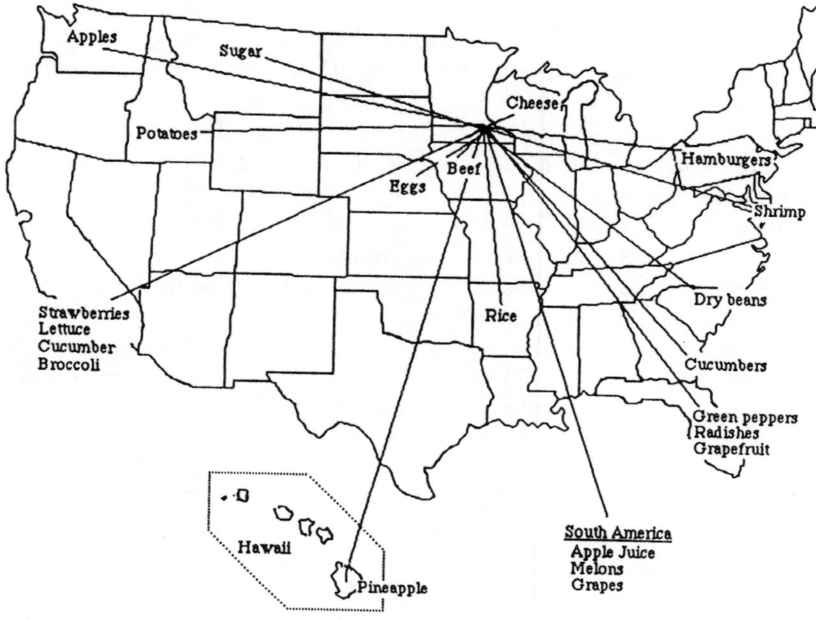

Note: Each college purchases about 19 percent of its food from in-state producers and 81 percent from out-of-state producers. Sources vary throughout each year. This map shows the states that supply the largest portions of the food items listed.

within a few years. An inquiry into local producers yielded several candidates: a pork producer who uses no antibiotics or hormones to stimulate growth; a beef and pork producer who uses similar methods; a milk-marketing organization that is trying to establish a market for certified organic milk (the two colleges' total dairy purchases amount to around 25 percent of the total demand necessary to establish a competitive, certified-organic milk market in Minnesota); and an apple grower who practices several methods of integrated pest management that reduce his pesticide use below that of his competitors.

Last year, trial purchases of the locally produced apples yielded uniformly excellent reviews from the students. After years of eating apples from Washington State trucked to Minnesota, it appears that for the coming years Carleton and Saint Olaf students will enjoy apples grown a short distance from the campuses. The price of these apples is competitive and the quality substantially better than "shipped-in" apples, judging from student reaction. Both food service directors and the apple grower are pleased with the arrangement. At the outset, the colleges' demand was greater than

Figure 9.2. Monthly Availability of Fresh Minnesota-Grown Produce

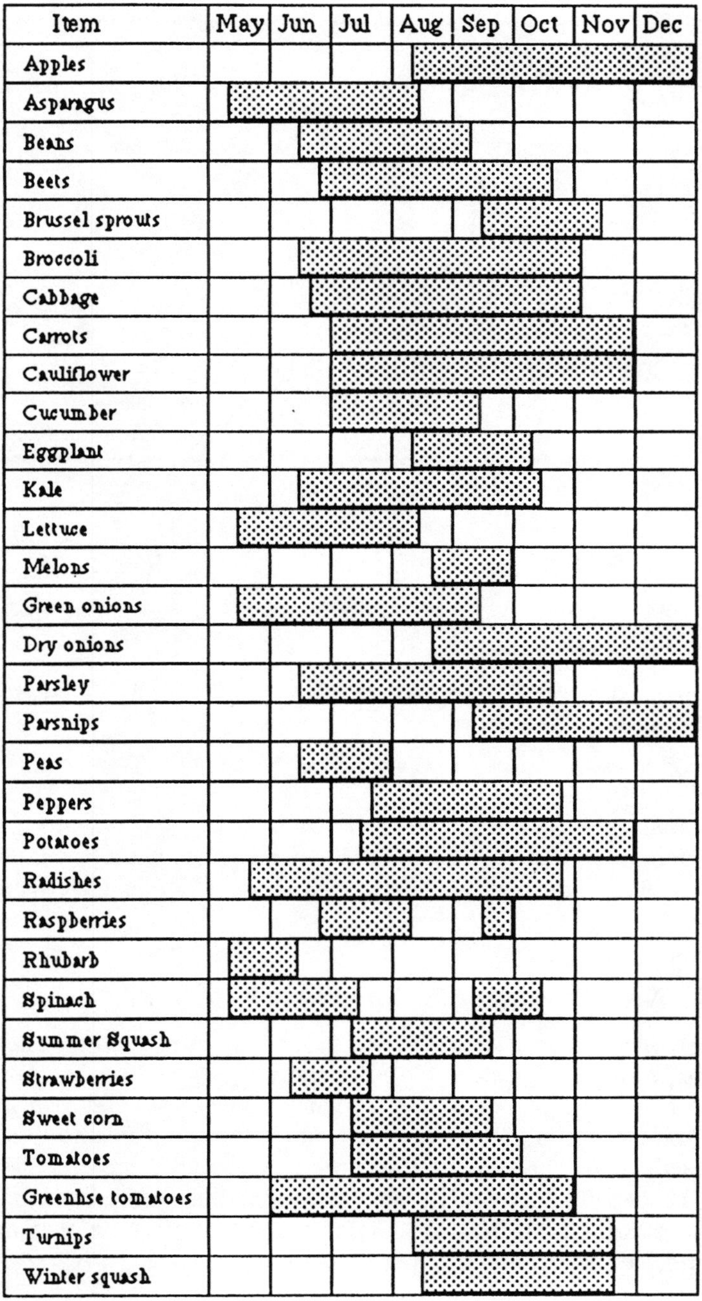

Item	May	Jun	Jul	Aug	Sep	Oct	Nov	Dec
Apples				▓	▓	▓	▓	▓
Asparagus	▓	▓						
Beans		▓	▓	▓				
Beets			▓	▓	▓			
Brussel sprouts					▓	▓		
Broccoli		▓	▓	▓	▓			
Cabbage			▓	▓	▓	▓		
Carrots			▓	▓	▓	▓		
Cauliflower			▓	▓	▓	▓		
Cucumber			▓	▓				
Eggplant				▓	▓			
Kale		▓	▓	▓	▓			
Lettuce	▓	▓	▓	▓				
Melons				▓	▓			
Green onions	▓	▓	▓	▓				
Dry onions				▓	▓	▓	▓	▓
Parsley		▓	▓	▓	▓	▓		
Parsnips					▓	▓	▓	▓
Peas		▓	▓					
Peppers			▓	▓	▓			
Potatoes			▓	▓	▓	▓		
Radishes	▓	▓	▓	▓				
Raspberries			▓	▓	▓			
Rhubarb	▓							
Spinach	▓	▓	▓	▓	▓			
Summer Squash			▓	▓	▓			
Strawberries		▓	▓					
Sweet corn			▓	▓	▓			
Tomatoes			▓	▓	▓			
Greenhse tomatoes		▓	▓	▓	▓	▓		
Turnips				▓	▓	▓	▓	
Winter squash				▓	▓	▓		

Figure 9.3. Energy Use in Food Storage Processes and Transportation

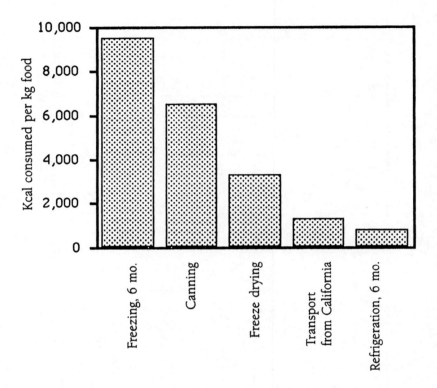

Note: Energy values are kilogram calories celsius (Kcal) consumed per kilogram (kg) of food.

the local supply, but the grower's efforts to expand production, and his experimentation with hybrids that keep longer under refrigeration, are bringing supply up to the colleges' total demand for much of the school year.

Broader View of Minnesota Agriculture

A search of the literature on the topic and a series of discussions with officials from the Minnesota Department of Agriculture revealed pronounced changes in Minnesota agriculture over the past two decades. Farms have gotten bigger (Figure 9.4), fewer (Figure 9.5), and less diverse than they were in the past, and the trend continues. The years 1979–1987 saw a 12 percent increase through consolidation in the average size of Minnesota farms, with the gain coming at the loss of 12 percent, or twelve thousand, family farms—four per day—during that eight-year period. As

Figure 9.4. Average Size of
Farms in Minnesota, 1979–1988

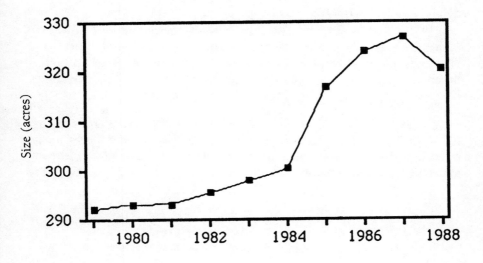

Figure 9.5. Number of Farms
in Minnesota, 1979–1988

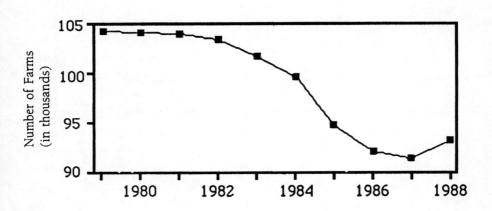

shown in Figures 9.4 and 9.5, the changes in curve slopes in 1988 should not be viewed as the end of the trend; corporate farms have an incentive to divide their assets on paper so as to capture several times over the federal payments targeted at small farms.

The consolidation is characterized by monocropping on individual farms, low crop diversity in the region, and extensive use of agricultural chemicals. Of the three dozen or so crops now commonly grown in Minnesota, the top four crops (feed corn, soybeans, alfalfa, and wheat) dominate, taking 87 percent of the land under cultivation. Inclusion of the next four crops (barley, oats, sugarbeets, and sweet corn) brings the acreage to more than 97 percent of the total (Figure 9.6), with all other crops taking less than 3 percent of the cultivated land (Figure 9.7). For colleges interested in a diverse menu, this large scale and low diversity of mainstream agriculture are impediments to local buying.

Figure 9.6. Acres of Major Crops Harvested Annually in Minnesota

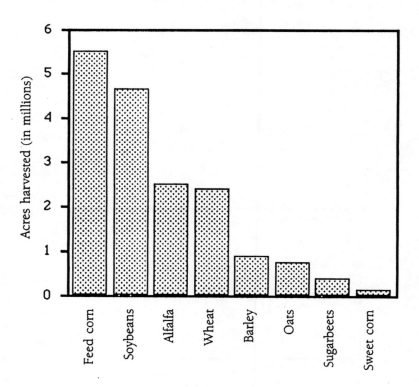

Figure 9.7. Acres of Minor Crops Harvested Annually in Minnesota

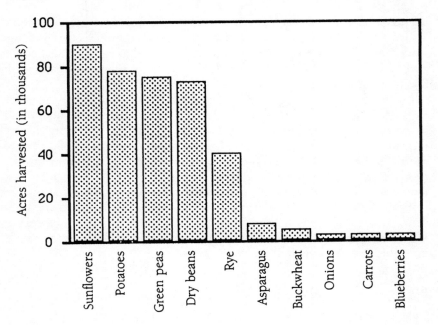

Ancillary Concerns

Complexity and difficulty in getting complete information prevented the students from directly connecting the colleges' use of a particular food to any single agrichemical problem. Their review of the literature on agricultural chemicals did, however, reveal cause for concern and support an argument for buying food locally from growers with whom we could deal personally.

The students found that during the growing season, a full spectrum of pesticides is in midwestern public water supply systems, a direct result of pesticide-laden agricultural runoff entering surface waters. Minnesota's aquifers contain more than a dozen pesticides year-round, and it is unusual to find a groundwater sample that is not contaminated with agricultural chemicals. Although in most cases the levels of contamination are below the maximum limits set by the U.S. Environmental Protection Agency, the synergistic effects on humans of combining two or more of these chemicals are largely unknown. The story is repeated in every agricultural state, with possible commensurate human health problems and broader problems of land and water degradation.

To the students, these potential connections between the college and agrichemical pollution raised questions of ethics and consistency. Can educational institutions that purport to challenge students to "develop a philosophy of life," and to be "responsible and knowledgeable citizens of the world," accept their position in economic systems that concentrate benefits and spread costs? How do colleges demonstrate the values that they would like their students to embrace?

The students' interest in the true costs of their food was not entirely altruistic. They learned about the "Delaney clause," which explicitly prohibits carcinogenic food additives, and how loopholes in this federal legislation can allow carcinogenic pesticides into food. A look at meat and dairy production revealed that antibiotics, used at low doses in healthy animals to stimulate production, also promote the development of antibiotic-resistant strains of bacteria, particularly salmonella. It was such an antibiotic-resistant strain that caused the outbreak of nearly two-hundred thousand serious cases of salmonellosis in 1985. This was the largest outbreak in U.S. history, traced to contamination at a single Illinois dairy, reminding us again of why we should all know our growers.

Financing Local Buying

Having justified the buy-local-and-sustainable plan in principle, the students faced the remaining hurdle of figuring a way to pay for the plan. Although it carries the benefits of reduced pesticide use, reduced soil erosion, and a healthier, more resilient economy, sustainable agriculture does not always produce inexpensive food. The students found that almost any initiative to redirect food purchases would cost the colleges extra money, at least in the short run, and that to pass muster with the administrations, they would have to find a way to help the colleges make up at least part of the difference.

How does one raise funds for a local food project? Raise tuition? Cut faculty salaries? Trim the administration? We needed to find an existing budget that everyone would agree was too big and that, when cut, would advance the broader goals of the program.

The energy budget proved to fit these criteria. Working primarily at Saint Olaf, two students on the program staff worked during summer 1990 devising a plan to replace inefficient lighting fixtures in two buildings with energy-efficient fixtures. A test area in each of two buildings demonstrated the acceptability of the fixtures, and careful accounting illustrated their cost-effectiveness. The preferred retrofits were shown to save 75 percent and 87 percent, respectively, of the preretrofit lighting energy, to yield a real internal rate of return (above inflation) of 61 percent and 101 percent annually and to reduce annual electric bills by over $4,000 and $3,000, respectively. With the agreement of the administrations, part of the financial savings (after subtracting the cost of the retrofits) were used to help finance the local-buying initiative.

While these financial savings offer the local food program a boost, additional benefits include reduced energy imports (Minnesota imports almost all of its energy at considerable cost), a reduction of two hundred tons per year of carbon dioxide emissions from coal-fired power plants, and the related improvement of air quality. Each of these benefits is entirely consistent with the broader goal of building a sustainable agricultural economy in Minnesota. In that context, the energy study was a particularly rewarding way for the students to wrap up their research. Discouraged by a budget constraint, the students were able to ease that constraint while helping, in a small but important way, to ease the colleges' burdens on the environment.

Regional Conference

To encourage other colleges to join in our local buying effort and to learn how other colleges have approached these issues, the Campus and the Biosphere initiative sponsored a two-day conference at Saint Olaf in spring 1991. The conference brought together faculty, food service directors, physical plant directors, and students to discuss campus environmental concerns relevant to their areas of campus involvement. In total, 130 people representing twenty-nine colleges and ten farms and farm-related organizations participated.

Although local growing for local consumption was the primary focus, the conference also addressed related topics such as recycling and energy conservation in the context of a broader discussion of environmental education by participation and example. David W. Orr, April A. Smith, and Gary L. Valen (all contributors to this volume) shared their experiences at Oberlin College, the University of California at Los Angeles, and Hendrix College, respectively—experiences that served in part as the basis for integrated discussions that brought faculty, students, administrators, and staff together in a unique and productive way.

At the outset of our work it was mainly idealistic students and faculty who set out to "show" the system how to change, but it was the patience and understanding contributions of full-time college staff, including the food service and the physical plant directors, who did much of the educating of the students and faculty. Through the full-time personnel, we learned of the practical constraints that the students would subsequently encounter. This practical learning acquired from the study of a "real" system was perhaps the most important immediate gain of the project and conference. We need more of these kinds of experiences at our academic institutions.

Several faculty at the conference thought that there would be administrative resistance to substantial environmental investigations on their campuses. Our experience has been that there is little resistance when the administration, staff, and faculty all understand and participate in the process. This participation is not difficult to achieve but does require forethought and cooperation. The importance of the involvement of the food service and the physical plant directors in our own work is difficult to overstate.

Continuing Efforts and Continued Learning

The objective of our current work is to bring local growers, food distributors, and college food service directors together in an effort to identify locally grown products that can be funneled through local food distributors. This effort requires a large enough volume and steady supply (at least on a seasonal basis) of produce from the growers. It also requires a commitment from the food distributors to handle the commodities, as well as a commitment from the colleges to purchase the products, even if the costs are slightly higher than what they are accustomed to paying.

The process is slow because it depends in part on having traditional growers of feed corn and soybeans shift from large-scale monocrops to more diverse crops suitable for direct human consumption. Unfortunately, many farmers who saw neighbors lose their land during the 1980s are reluctant to risk a new venture. The pressure against change is made even stronger by government incentives that encourage monocropping of grain for feed. It appears that the most attractive possibilities are with small growers who are already selling to local markets. The challenge is to bring a sufficient number of these growers together with several large buyers (including the colleges) to ensure steady flows of produce.

We measure the successes of the Campus and the Biosphere initiative in several ways. The students identified viable options for purchasing locally and sustainably produced food, and we now continue with the gradual process of realizing those options. Through the regional conference, we involved several other colleges in our effort to buy locally, expanding the realm of alternatives. We are cultivating this broader base of interest through a series of meetings, recognizing that the combined buying power of many colleges, as opposed to just two, is needed to establish local markets.

The project has been educational for students, faculty, and the administrations. No textbooks were necessary; indeed, the students wrote their own curriculum. They grappled with the pressing problems of agriculture, searched for answers, and found them. It was not as easy or as rapid as they had expected, but the answers that they produced reflect persistence, imagination, and a genuine concern for the causes that they advanced.

EUGENE B. BAKKO is professor of biology at Saint Olaf College, Northfield, Minnesota, and the Saint Olaf adviser to the Campus and the Biosphere initiative.

JOHN C. WOODWELL is former manager of the program and is currently a master's degree student in resource economics at Duke University, School of Forestry and Environmental Studies, Durham, North Carolina.

On campuses around the country, student groups are discovering the benefits of working on projects in cooperation with campus officials.

Student Environmental Organizations

Julian Keniry, Brian Trelstad

In April 1989, the National Wildlife Federation initiated the Cool It! program, a nationwide challenge to college students, faculty, and administrators to hold themselves and their institutions accountable for their share of the wasteful practices degrading our natural world. Equipped with the lessons learned from our own campus projects as undergraduates, we joined Cool It! to help students elsewhere develop effective environmental programs on their campuses. Since then, we, along with seven other staff members, have visited over two hundred campuses and have been in contact with students, faculty, and administrators on over one thousand colleges and universities across the country.

We have been taught some clear lessons from this constant interaction with students and staff. From those that wage emotional debates about 1960s radicalism to those that propose complicated plans to reduce campus energy consumption, we have drawn conclusions about the different types of environmental groups on college campuses. We have also learned what works and what does not. In the course of this chapter, we document the successes and shortcomings of some of these programs and articulate what we believe are the most salient lessons from them.

Changing Traditions of Student Environmentalism

The last three years have witnessed the transformation of student environmentalism. Traditionally linked with 1960s activism, the environmentalists of today are a varied and evolving group. From Earth Day 1970 to the establishment of the Student Environmental Action Coalition (SEAC), a national grassroots student environmental network formed in 1988, campus activists have moved from being idealistic to being idealistic and effective.

The first widespread involvement of college students in the environmental movement came with the first Earth Day in 1970. Intending to direct the energy of student antiwar activism toward the environment, Senator Gaylord Nelson and Denis Hayes, a Harvard law student, organized a national event that involved thousands of students across the country and launched hundreds of local environmental campaigns. "Split Wood Not Atoms" became the environmental analogue to "Make Love Not War," and the environmental movement came to be seen as an integral part of the counterculture (Hays, 1987).

In fall 1989, Denis Hayes rekindled the old fires and catalyzed a reawakening of student environmentalism. For the twentieth anniversary of Earth Day, he made a concerted effort to organize and involve college campuses and to implement a straightforward plan: Bring together student environmentalists, offer them information and support networks, and direct them to organize large regional events.

The historical association between the first Earth Day and its anniversary, however, has raised many questions about the connection between the legacy of 1960s radicalism and student environmentalism today. Despite the obvious retrospectives linking Earth Day 1990 with that of 1970, SEAC has made the connection even stronger. For example, Tom Hayden, a founder of the Students for a Democratic Society, a national college coalition of peace activists during the 1960s, was a keynote speaker at the third annual SEAC conference, where the main theme was social justice and the environment.

While many students still operate in the shadow of the peace and civil rights movements (Miller, 1987), this legacy does not exclusively encompass all campus environmentalists today; rather, it merely describes some salient influences that we still encounter among many of these groups. We have also noticed that the legacy of the 1960s is both an asset and a liability to these groups.

The inspirational presence of 1960s idealism cannot be overlooked. One prominent SEAC organizer urges students to consider how small groups of people have changed the course of American history. Equating environmentalism with suffrage and civil rights, he advocates connecting issues of social justice with environmentalism. He represents many students who derive a strong source of commitment to social equality that they bring to their campuses. His group, the Cornell Greens, in Ithaca, New York, has forged strong ties with a local labor union in protesting the planned hydroelectric project James Bay II, as much for its effects on New York's economy and the rights of indigenous peoples as for its environmental impact. The increasing number of student coalitions with labor unions and grass-roots groups run by people of color attests these students' desire for diversity and inclusivity within environmentalism.

At the same time, however, the legacy of the 1960s has created political problems for student environmental groups. A rift between antiestablishment students and those willing to work within the system is perhaps wider than is generally recognized. For a business student preparing a cost-benefit analysis of a campus recycling proposal, the tension with classmates who plan direct actions against the local Exxon station is tangible. For those students who "question authority" and remain wary of hierarchical structures and bureaucrats in general, the legacy of the 1960s has made it difficult to approach administrators. And these misperceptions also work in the opposite direction. Memories of hostile student demands and abandoned recycling programs linger with campus administrators even today, making them suspicious of many student environmental initiatives.

In addition to the mutual misperceptions between students and administrators, many environmental groups today are hindered by lack of structure and are guided by students devoid of leadership skills. Student governments have traditionally provided enterprising and engaging students with leadership development training; campus environmental groups have not. A lack of organizational structures, combined with an aversion to constitutions and minute taking, has meant that student environmental groups have ebbed and flowed with the personalities of their members. In fact, each year the Cool It! staff receives several applications from "new groups" on campuses that only two years prior had active environmental organizations. Varying levels of commitment and enthusiasm from year to year have made it difficult to sustain environmental programs, leading administrators to be wary of the reliability of these groups.

This situation is changing, however. Increasing numbers of the students that we work with are "mainstream," and the legacy of the 1960s is becoming more of an asset than a liability. The powerful social vision remains, but the organizational and leadership skills are improving. In addition to Cool It! and SEAC, other national groups have played a growing role in the development of environmental student leaders.

The state coordinators of SEAC and the regional offices of Earth Day 1990 created a powerful national network. In the four years since its founding, evidenced by its annual national conferences with participation of at least fifteen hundred students each year (in October 1990, seven thousand students came to the University of Illinois, Champaign-Urbana), SEAC has become the most successful national student organization ever created. The publication of its monthly magazine, *Threshold,* and the growing number of subscriptions to Student EnviroLink, an international computer mailing list, have moved student environmentalism from isolated campus rallies to a formidable political front.

The efforts of Cool It! differ from those of SEAC in that we have not promoted specific issues or spent much time organizing around legislative initiatives. Instead, our niche is in working with students to develop leadership skills and staff who are interested in making their campuses models of environmentally sound practices. By focusing on the campus, we have, through our programs, taken the maxim "Think Globally, Act Locally" to colleges and universities. We have also devoted a considerable amount of our resources to developing the leadership skills of the students with whom we work, performing workshops on setting goals, and providing guides to campus organizing.

Other national environmental groups have responded to the growing demand for information on college campuses. The Union of Concerned Scientists created an organizing packet on global warming. The Public Interest Research Groups have focused much of their campus outreach on environmental initiatives. The Rainforest Action Network has formed Rainforest Action Groups on over one hundred campuses, providing them with information on effective ways to help protect the tropics.

This heightened awareness and the availability of our (and other groups') resources have brought a greater diversity of student groups into the movement. Student governments, fraternities, historically black colleges and universities, and community colleges have been some of the more active groups that have worked with Cool It! As an outgrowth of the legacy of 1960s radicalism, the changes on campus since Earth Day 1990 have given these groups a new legitimacy on college and university campuses. And though campus environmental groups take many forms, there are patterns in the way that they go about their business and in what happens over time.

Patterns in Student Environmental Groups: Notes from the Field

Against the changing backdrop of campus environmentalism, we are often asked to tell a group where it stands relative to other groups. From our many trips to colleges and universities and our daily telephone discussions with new and old groups, it is clear that most fall into one of three general categories: students interested in educating themselves and their classmates, students who develop independent environmental projects, and student-administrative coalitions that work on sustainable campus change. The following examples from around the country serve to sharpen this rough typology of campus groups that has helped us understand how we can work with them effectively.

The Rush to Inform. At the beginning of each academic semester, we receive scores of letters and telephone calls from students who convey one form or another of the following message: "The primary objective of our group is to increase awareness. Any information or ideas for Earth Week would be . . . helpful." This example from Cumberland College, in Williamsburg, Kentucky, joins hundreds of other examples of students who request our help in setting up informational campaigns on national and global issues. "Apathy" is often cited as the problem that the proposed forums and films are supposed to address. Yet, in November 1989, when the National Wildlife Federation conducted a survey to "assess awareness and concern for environmental issues on America's campuses" (Hughes Research Corporation, 1989, p. 1), 50 percent of the students polled indicated that they were more concerned about environmental problems than were their classmates. The concern is clearly there; however, the ability to tap it is in question.

Cool It! responds to the informational needs of these student groups, but we often find that apathy is a misdiagnosis of the problem. While we do supply organizing materials and respond to requests for information, it is difficult to find a proper balance between making suggestions and accommodating our callers. We have overwhelmed more than a few students by suggesting that they do a waste stream analysis or that they approach administrators. Our hope in assisting with educational campaigns is that our informational materials will prompt action on the issues and on the scale that leaders deem appropriate.

Whether or not the accumulation and sharing of information leads to action, this process represents a key lesson of environmental organizing: Recognize the importance and availability of existing off-campus resources. Once students begin to navigate the revolutionized world of information and communication, they can soon take advantage of a variety of powerful organizing tools. From Cool It!'s issue packets and SEAC's regional committees, to computer bulletin boards such as Econet and Student Enviro-Link, national resources exist for students. Students who are aware of these resources have learned the first lesson of campus organizing.

Ideals into Action. Environmental organizations that make the connection between national environmental problems and campus resource use form the second general category of student groups. By linking the issues of global warming to recycling, for example, or the building of a local hydroelectric plant with energy efficiency, these groups develop focused goals and put ideas into action. While aware of off-campus resources, these groups tend to strike out on their own, ignoring the resources that exist on campus. The shortcomings and successes of their programs lead to one of two outcomes: the disillusionment of the students with an accompanying loss of faith from the administration or the beginning of steadily expanding environmental programs on campus. But students learn valuable grass-roots organizing skills regardless of the outcome.

A classic example of the operational methods of a group of this kind occurred at Agnes Scott College, in Decatur, Georgia. Recognizing the link between the national landfill crisis and the campus waste stream, the ecology club, GAIA, began to devise a recycling program. Typical of many volunteer environmental groups, they started to plan the program without consulting the administration or talking to people on other campuses who had coordinated successful programs. Charging ahead with idealism and enthusiasm, the students put out bins and wrote a plan for monitoring and emptying them. Not until the bins began to overflow with recyclables did the students look for help. The director of business affairs allowed a trailer for newspaper to be kept in a parking lot, and the director of student activities found space for other materials in the student center. But the unanticipated volume of materials collected when students moved out of their dormitory rooms left a few volunteers with the overwhelming task of separating and hauling a couple of tons of newspaper, glass, and aluminum.

Labor-intensive programs such as this recycling effort lead to high rates of burnout and, often, abrupt ends to the projects. At Mississippi State University, student volunteers in a group called SCAPE abandoned their ambitious aluminum, newspaper, computer paper, and glass recycling program established in fall 1990. According to a student coordinator, the campus dean was not approached about campus resources until volunteers decided that they needed help developing an incentive system to hold group members accountable for the monitoring and emptying of bins. Ironically, it was then that the students discovered a center for recycling research on their own campus, which was in the process of developing a program for Mississippi State and disseminating recycling information to other public schools and state agencies. Student involvement in the environmental group at Mississippi State waned after the failure of their efforts to initiate recycling, but it has accelerated again since student organizers attended the national SEAC conference and refocused their efforts. The Agnes Scott initiative, however, has thrived. Students there now work on a variety of projects from composting to the procurement of recycled paper products.

The students at these two institutions learned the second lesson of successful campus organizing: Focus on a specific environmental problem and trace it back to the campus. The task of reducing overwhelming statistics about global warming or landfill crises to concrete actions designed for the campus is an empowering process. The failure to communicate well with the administration notwithstanding, these students made some strides in converting idealism to pragmatism. They also moved closer toward understanding their potential role as agents of campus environmental change.

A Team Effort. Students who recognize the valuable allies and resources that exist on their own campuses form the most advanced category of student groups. Adept at working campus political circles, they have an ability to develop far-reaching programs that have dramatic, campuswide impacts. In addition, students learn from cooperation with administrators, and vice versa, as both sides work to understand each other's roles in institutional change.

An innovative project at Harvard University demonstrates how beneficial a student-administration relationship can be in the development of
sustainable campus projects. The Ecolympics program, an energy conservation competition between dormitories developed by students and campus
personnel, reduced energy consumption by 25 percent over the course of
the year 1990–1991 (a savings of over $500,000 to the college), leading
Yale, Tufts, and the University of Wisconsin at Madison, among others, to
develop similar programs (Trelstad, 1991).

In spring 1990, students at Harvard University met with the director
of physical operations to discuss measures that the college was taking to
save energy. Recognizing that the Harvard administration had already made
a commitment to conserve resources on campus, the students suggested
starting an energy conservation competition. The following fall, anticipating
energy consumption increases and a jump in oil prices due to the impend-
ing Persian Gulf War, the director called another meeting with the students,
who had just completed a proposal for the Ecolympics.

They first discussed the campus resources available and the potential
impact of the program, both educationally and financially. The administration committed $5,000 in seed money and provided information (the meter
records for each building for each month over the past three years). The
students brought to the table their enthusiasm as volunteers and their
desire to develop a creative campaign. This combination of resources
offered the administration the much needed people-hours required to run
this kind of conservation program; it also gave the environmental group
the financial backing and administrative commitment needed to extend
the issue of energy conservation to the entire college.

The planning committee spent an equal amount of time developing
the logistics and the media strategy for the campaign. To compare the
monthly consumption in each dormitory from year to year, students created
a conservation index for each building. Residents in buildings that saved
the most in each of the resource areas would then be rewarded at the end
of each month; one final winner for the year would also be chosen.

With the Ecolympics as the main promotional theme, the program
vaulted from the obscurity of the committee meetings to the front page of
campus newspapers. Serving Rainforest Crunch ice cream at the awards
ceremonies, and presenting representatives from the winning house with
green hats and green socks, the student organizers—dressed in togas and
trumpeting the Olympic theme song—created more public awareness about
the campaign than had been anticipated. The students managed to package
the program so successfully that by the end of the school year 98 percent
of students polled knew about the program. The financial resources committed by the facilities office were essential, but the students, through their
own creativity and energy in using the money, were vital to the success of
the program.

Harvard's Ecolympics program demonstrates that students can master organizing skills and that faculty and staff do care about resource conservation. The savings achieved by the program encouraged the administration to allocate some of the money saved to the purchase of five hundred energy-efficient lightbulbs for students and to support the program for a second year. The success of the program created a dialogue between students and administrators that may lead to other collaborative initiatives in years to come.

Another example of student-administration cooperation is the xeriscaping program at Mesa Community College, in Mesa, Arizona. For the last three years, students and staff at Mesa Community College have gradually converted nonrecreational turf to native Sonoran desert habitat. The natural landscaping attracts wildlife and requires little water and almost no expensive fertilizers and pesticides. What was once flat turf with a few palm trees and junipers is fast becoming a complex ecosystem, providing a living laboratory for students across disciplines and local organizations (SEAC, p. 60).

The educational benefits and financial savings resulting from xeriscaping (outweighing the few hundred dollars that the program cost to convert the land) would not have been realized without student involvement and administrative commitment. According to the cochair of the Xeriscaping Committee, the dean of student services was instrumental in granting faculty release time to maintain and document the program. The head of campus grounds has assisted grounds staff in the transition out of heavy equipment, irrigation, and spraying. Life sciences faculty made the study and restoration of the habitat an integral part of the curriculum. And students have been the backbone of the program, providing enthusiastic labor that the college otherwise could not have afforded. Students and staff have started developing ideas for extending the momentum into other issue areas such as campus recycling and food service policy.

Other examples of positive administrative response to student initiative abound. At Patrick Henry Community College in Martinsville, Virginia, the director of college relations paid for the printing and mailing of materials for a statewide environmental conference sponsored by ECOS, an environmental committee of the student government. And at the College of William and Mary, in Williamsburg, Virginia, the director of business affairs hired the student who had been lobbying him to replace disposables with permanent dishware to coordinate the college's recycling program (Cool It!, 1991).

Where students have been persistent, they have learned the third lesson of campus organizing: Use of existing campus resources and establishment of coalitions with administrators help to build stronger, more sustainable campus programs. The involvement of physical plant, food service, and financial staff has been instrumental in most successful campus programs.

And those campuses that establish a working dialogue between students and administrators can begin to think about the fourth and final lesson of campus environmentalism: It is important to plan for the long term.

Lessons from the Past, Challenges for the Future

The majority of the groups with whom Cool It! works belong in the middle category of our typology. They are trying to put their ideals into action and we offer assistance in information and leadership development that many students find helpful. Few strong campus models exist, but we are beginning to document the team efforts that have had a demonstrable impact on their respective campuses. For those groups that are just beginning the process of environmental organizing, we offer the four basic lessons articulated in this chapter: (1) Learn about existing national resources, (2) focus on specific issues and concrete campus actions, (3) recognize the resources on campus and work with the administration in taking advantage of them, and (4) plan for the long term with an eye toward sustainability.

The wealth and diversity of campus resources and expertise lead us to believe that together, students and administrators have an opportunity to develop model environmental programs on college campuses. These synergistic relationships can broaden the scope and elevate the efficacy of sustainable environmental projects, making them an integral part of campus life. Yet, student-based initiatives are not without their shortcomings. Limited by their two- or four-year stays on campus, students are often rendered powerless when it comes to shaping campus policy. Thus, they gravitate toward projects that offer short-term results. Administrators are needed to infuse the programs with elements of long-range planning.

Despite these limitations, campus environmental projects offer excellent learning opportunities for students. The opportunities to study resource use and local ecosystems, to draft policy and press releases, and to interact with members of the faculty, staff, and community coalesce into an experiential education nonpareil. The stronger the student networks grow and the greater the resources that are available, the more the students will be able to make this kind of practical activism a vital aspect of their college education.

References

Cool It! *Students Working for a Sustainable World: The Cool It! Project Directory.* Washington, D.C.: National Wildlife Federation, 1991.

Hayes, Samuel P. *Beauty, Health, and Permanence.* New York: Cambridge University Press, 1987.

Hughes Research Corporation. *Planet in Peril: A View from the Campus.* Washington, D.C.: National Wildlife Federation, 1989.

Miller, James. *Democracy Is in the Streets.* New York: Simon & Schuster, 1987.

Student Environmental Action Coalition. *The Student Environmental Action Guide.* Berkeley, Calif.: EarthWorks Press, 1991.

Trelstad, Brian. *Ecolympics Project Report.* Washington, D.C.: National Wildlife Federation, 1991.

JULIAN KENIRY *is campus environmental audit specialist for Cool It! of the National Wildlife Federation, Washington, D.C. She has worked there since graduating from Agnes Scott College, Decatur, Georgia, in 1989, where she cofounded the campus environmental group GAIA. She is a member of an Environmental Protection Agency task force of the Pollution Prevention Education Committee.*

BRIAN TRELSTAD *is northeast regional coordinator of Cool It! He graduated from Harvard University in 1991, where he cofounded and codirected the Ecolympics program.*

The broad appeal of recycling makes it the most widespread and popular campus environmental activity, but it is not without its own challenges and environmental consequences.

Campus Recycling: Everyone Plays a Part

Raymond Ching, Robert Gogan

Recycling is becoming a way of life for most North American colleges and universities. To date, forty-eight states and several urban areas of Canada have enacted mandatory recycling legislation. Rising disposal costs, shrinking landfill space, concerns about incineration, and legislative mandates have led campuses to separate their trash for recycling (Watson, 1990). Environmental activism among students and staff has also sparked the implementation of recycling programs. The following three examples illustrate this trend: (1) Each member of the Board of Trustees of Michigan State University, in East Lansing, received a copy of a petition with thousands of signatures demanding that undergraduates be given an opportunity to recycle their newspapers and used beverage containers in their dormitories. Within three months, every dormitory got recycling pickup service. (2) Over one hundred students and staff at Dartmouth College, in Hanover, New Hampshire, carried their personal trash around campus for one week in a graphic demonstration of individuals' contributions to the waste stream. Their transparent bags gradually filled with newspapers, food packaging, and junk mail, showing how much trash college students and staff generate in their daily routines. The Dartmouth recycling program was able to recycle three of the five truckloads collected during the "Trashcapade" (Janiak, 1990). (3) Laboratory technicians at Harvard Medical School gave up valuable floor space to stockpile used, nonhazardous, plastic laboratory implements for recycling. Within six months, the plant maintenance department provided custodial service for plastics collection, set aside storage space, and paid for weekly recycling pickup service.

In this chapter, we outline the range of campus recycling models, describe how recycling fits in with an overall solid waste management strategy, and highlight important issues in planning for recycling. Data on recycling programs at ten representative institutions are presented in Table 11.1 as a quick reference

NEW DIRECTIONS FOR HIGHER EDUCATION, no. 77, Spring 1992 © Jossey-Bass Publishers

Table 11.1. Highlights of Select College and University Recycling Programs

Campus, Location, Contact	Student/Total Campus Population	Materials Recycled	Tons of Recyclables (Most Recent Annual Data Available)	Evolution of Program
Brown University Providence, R.I. James Corless (401) 863-7837	6,500/9,500	OCC, ONP, MX, WL, MC, P, food waste, leaves, wood, scrap metals	497	1986: Student volunteers 1988: Institutionalized
University of Colorado Boulder, Colo. Jack DeBell (303) 497-8307	25,571/30,771	CL, CPO, OCC, ONP, OPB, WL, A-UBC, P, yard waste, polystyrene packaging, laser cartridges, scrap metal	761	1976: Student volunteers 1984: Institutionalized
Denison University Granville, Ohio Matt Harvey (614) 587-6264	1,900/2,150	CL, CPO, OCC, ONP, WL, G, MC, P, hard-cover books	985	1986: Student volunteers 1988: Institutionalized
Harvard University Cambridge, Mass. Robert Gogan (617) 495-3042	17,000/27,000	CL, CPO, OCC, ONP, OPB, WL, G, MC, P, C&D, leaves, pallets	1092	1971: Local staff and student volunteers 1990: Institutionalized
University of Illinois Urbana–Champaign, Ill. Tim Hoss (217) 244-7283	34,260/38,030	CL, CPO, OMG, ONP, WL, MC, P, pallets, brush, fats and cooking oils, leaves, lead-acid batteries, motor oil, scrap metal, tires	2,330 (excludes fats and cooking oils)	1981: Voluntary local efforts 1989: Institutionalized
University of Michigan Ann Arbor, Mich. Buck Marks (313) 763-5534	36,475/60,475	MX, WL, OCC, ONP, G, P, C&D, leaves, pallets, scrap metal	2,457	1981: Volunteers 1989: Institutionalized

Institution	Tonnage	Total recyclables	Items	History
University of Minnesota, Twin Cities Minneapolis-St. Paul, Minn. Dana Donatucci (612) 624-8507	58,570/75,570	2,555	CL, CPO, OCC, ONP, WL, MC, P, C&D, dry-cell batteries, lead-acid batteries, pallets, scrap metals, yard waste	1970: Volunteers 1983: Institutionalized
Rutgers, the State University of New Jersey New Brunswick, N.J. Raymond Ching (908) 937-5858	32,000/41,000	2,460 (excludes engine oil)	CL, CPO, OMG, ONP, WL, commingled MC and G and P, C&D, leaves, livestock grade food waste, used engine oil, yard waste	1972: Student volunteers 1987: Institutionalized
Stanford University Palo Alto, Calif. Stanford Public Information Office Heidi Clark (415) 723-0919	13,360/14,685	1,950	CL, CPO, junk mail, OCC, OMG, ONP, WL, G, MC, P, yard waste	1977: Student volunteers 1985: Institutionalized
Stockton State College Pomona, N.J. Scott Mauger (609) 652-4221	5,240/5,890	189	OCC, ONP, WL, A-UBC, G, MC, fats and oils, lead-acid batteries, tires, scrap metals, yard waste	1974: Student volunteers 1988: Institutionalized

Note: The data represent self-reported information or estimates. Items listed in the third column are arranged by proportional weight of recyclables, in descending order. Criteria for determining tonnage counts may differ between schools, for example, some campuses include leaves in total, others do not. Contact campus coordinators directly for questions. Key to abbreviations: A = aluminum, C&D = construction and demolition debris, CL = colored ledger (for example, copier paper and stationery), CPO = computer printouts, G = glass jars and bottles, MC = metal cans, MX = mixed office paper, OCC = old corrugated containers (for example, cardboard copier paper boxes), OMG = old magazines, ONP = old newsprint, OPB = old phone books, UBC = used beverage containers, WL = white ledger paper.

guide to the issues and materials discussed in this chapter. In Exhibit 11.1, we provide nutshell descriptions of the programs at these same ten institutions.

The National Scene

Campus recycling programs run the spectrum from local volunteer efforts to official or institutionalized campuswide recycling infrastructures. The programs may target aluminum cans, various grades of paper, leaves and yard waste, glass, metal, plastic, food waste, motor oil, construction and demolition debris, or any other discarded material for which a local market exists. Recycling often begins as a volunteer effort and grows into an officially sponsored service; campus-specific factors such as proximity to markets, ease of collection, and local landfill rates influence this evolution (Ching and Coston, 1990). Some campuses, such as the University of Rochester in New York, first relied on a handful of dedicated staff volunteers but have since hired recycling coordinators. Student volunteers initiated and still coordinate recycling at other campuses, such as California Polytechnic State University, in San Luis Obispo, where students also chose to use bicycle carts to reduce the environmental impact of hauling operations.

Hybrid programs using paid employees as well as volunteers have evolved at other institutions. Stockton State College, in Pomona, New Jersey (see Table 11.1 and Exhibit 11.1), pays the student environmental organization to educate members of the campus community, manage collection within buildings, and coordinate pickup. This system links conveniently with Atlantic County's Materials Recovery Facility, which takes the bulk of the material away for processing and recycling. Massachusetts Institute of Technology, in Cambridge, relies on student volunteers to collect and prepare recyclables within each dormitory but pays a recycling service for weekly removal.

Most campuses eventually commit paid staff resources to recycling. Grass-roots programs often suffer from volunteer burnout, student departures during vacation periods, and accumulations of recyclables crowding out campus buildings when pickups are missed. At Harvard (see Table 11.1 and Exhibit 11.1), for instance, student volunteers succeeded in delivering commingled recyclables to the recycling transfer station but were unwilling to spend weekends in an icy, windswept parking lot sorting the material to market specifications. Consequently, unsorted recyclables grew into a sixty-cubic-yard heap that drew the scorn of the university administration and arson-fearing public safety officials—and offered an ideal habitat for the local rodent population. By the next fall, the campus Facilities Maintenance Department had taken over collection and sorting, eliminating the prospect of aesthetic or safety concerns due to unreliable volunteer performance. It was clear that if the university did not collect and ship out recyclable materials the right way, volunteers would do it the wrong way, with potentially disastrous consequences

Exhibit 11.1. Operational and Topical Details of Select College and University Recycling Programs

Brown University: Daily trash weight reports lead to accuracy in knowing recycling and trash tonnage ratios. The campus emphasizes cost avoidance. Brown's trash hauler provides tip fee rebates for recycling tonnage. Rhode Island mandates recycling at Brown (effective 1990). The environmental studies program engages students in research topics on campus recycling, providing waste audits, policy analysis, and other help.

University of Colorado, Boulder: On-campus markets for recyclables are used whenever possible to reduce hauling costs, for example, "U. of C. compost tea" is sold as houseplant fertilizer. The program emphasizes local grass-roots involvement. Boulder County helps fund operations. The campus disciplinary board credits recycling work toward community service time. The program demonstrates how environmental values can sustain recycling in the face of low landfill rates in the Rocky Mountain region. Building alterations or new construction now include space for storage and processing of recyclables. In April 1992, a five-thousand-square-foot materials recovery facility opened. Usable clothing, durable goods, and obsolete computers are donated to Third World countries. The program refers generators of motor-vehicle-related recyclables to off-campus markets.

Denison University: The ample cooperation from housekeeping and secretarial staff, fraternities, and physical plant staff makes the program thrive. The campus drop-off center is open to the surrounding community. The campus provides the town with a recycling site; the town helps the campus market recyclables; everybody wins.

Harvard University: The program evolved from localized, highly decentralized volunteer operations with 150 separate projects and twelve vendors to more efficient consolidation of facilities and marketing efforts. Local, unofficial programs still account for two-thirds of the recycling tonnage. Cambridge city ordinance mandates recycling in 1992. The medical facilities are recycling nonhazardous laboratory plastics.

University of Illinois, Urbana–Champaign: The university officially favors the purchase of products with recycled content. An on-campus transfer station offers the opportunity to recycle large items such as tree stumps, metal appliances, and pallets. Currently, the program recycles 40 percent of campus trash, nine years ahead of the state-mandated date.

University of Michigan: Dedicated university compactor trucks pick up recyclable materials and then take large loads directly to markets for maximum collection efficiency and minimum expense. Trash collection and recycling pickup are coordinated by the same office. A surcharge to fund recycling is assessed to each building's trash charges.

University of Minnesota: Well-designed outdoor stations offer one-stop recycling of newspaper, other paper, and used beverage containers and trash disposal. A compactor truck stops at dining halls and bookstores to pick up and crush corrugated cardboard for recycling, saving space inside buildings. The program serves 160 out of 208 campus buildings.

Exhibit 11.1. *(continued)*

Rutgers, the State University of New Jersey: Highly mechanized collection of trash and recyclables is achieved using front-loader trucks and color-coded dumpsters. Local markets with sorting facilities for mixed paper and commingled beverage containers reduce the waste generators' need to separate materials, encouraging maximum recycling participation. New Jersey has mandated recycling at Rutgers since 1987. The food waste recovery program sends over one thousand tons annually to contented dairy cows.

Stanford University: A campus drop-off center allows local residents to recycle conveniently at Stanford's expense. Curbside collection of trash and recyclables by a contracted hauler is provided in faculty and graduate student housing areas.

Stockton State College, Pomona, New Jersey: A student-initiated volunteer group (SAVE) took up the recycling cause in 1974 and kept it alive. The campus elected to subsidize SAVE to help run the institutionalized program. SAVE performs waste audits and provides recycling publicity and information to campus media services.

Institutionalization can quickly lead to better participation. If members of a campus community know that they can count on reliable service, they are more eager to take the trouble to set aside materials for recycling in their offices or buildings. Many college and university programs have doubled or tripled tonnages recycled once day-to-day operations are taken over by the administration.

Integrating Recycling into a Waste Management Strategy

Campus trash management involves far more than dumping everything into the nearest landfill. According to most states' environmental protection departments, responsible solid waste management involves a hierarchy of choices (Baxter and others, 1990). The preferable approach, of course, is to reduce, reuse, recycle, and compost waste before resorting to incineration and landfilling. Examples of common source reduction methods at colleges and universities include using automatic double-side copying machines, favoring vendors who deliver their products with less packaging, using washable dishware, converting to microscale chemistry laboratories, printing fewer copies of campus newspapers, and discouraging delivery of unsolicited mailings, telephone directories, and giveaway newspapers. Source reduction is particularly cost-effective in hazardous waste management. At colleges and universities with lots of waste from clinics or research laboratories, this practice is increasingly common.

An especially popular campus waste reduction measure is the use of refillable plastic coffee mugs. Insulated plastic mugs emblazoned with campus insignia and earth-friendly slogans have appeared at hundreds of institutions, greatly reducing purchase and disposal costs of polystyrene

foam or plastic-coated paper cups and lids (paper hot cups cost three to seven cents each). Potsdam College in New York cut consumption of disposable hot drink cups by 58 percent in a one-year period after implementing a mug program (Student Environmental Action Coalition, 1991, p. 12). The Wisconsin Union of the University of Wisconsin, in Madison, sold over twenty-one thousand mugs, at two dollars apiece, in the first two years (1989–1991) of its program, saving the expense and environmental impact of manufacture, purchase, and disposal of hundreds of thousands of single-use cups and lids. The union offers a discount on hot beverages to mug-toting patrons.

Many campuses have discovered that reuse is also an effective waste management option. The practice of prolonging the useful life of a product or material also delays disposal and replacement costs. Options for reuse include rebuilding or reusing pallets, refilling laser printer toner cartridges, recirculating used furniture, and reusing foam polystyrene packing peanuts. By eliminating the volume of waste on campus, both reduction and reuse offer environmental and economic benefits.

When waste cannot be avoided, recycling and composting are the waste management options of choice. The significant role of recycling in reducing waste disposal tonnage is seen at Rutgers, the State University of New Jersey (see Table 11.1 and Exhibit 11.1), which has one of the oldest programs in the country. Out of a total 7,232 tons generated by the university in the 1990 calendar year, 2,460 tons or 34 percent were recycled, leaving only 4,768 tons to be hauled away.

Recycling also creates more jobs per dollar spent than do conventional trash disposal measures. Material must be transported, sorted, and processed separately. Recycling jobs also tend to be local. For example, Cornell University, in Ithaca, New York, has contracted with a sheltered workshop in the area to pick up and process recyclable paper waste (Hargett and Osborn, 1989). The universities of Minnesota and Colorado operate their own materials recovery facilities, employing dozens of students (see Table 11.1 and Exhibit 11.1).

Environmental benefits of recycling are clear. According to the National Wildlife Federation, recycling of one aluminum can saves the energy equivalent of six ounces (half of a can) of gasoline over manufacturing of a can from virgin materials. Recycling of one ton of paper saves seventeen thirty-foot trees and uses half the water and energy of virgin paper production. Recycling of a glass bottle saves enough energy to run a color television for four hours.

In addition, the practice of asking campus members to think before they discard their trash encourages a personal sense of frugality and efficient resource management. Everyone from the president to occasional visitors can participate. Recycling thus offers members of the campus community a concrete method for reducing environmental impacts of campus purchasing practices—a way to implement locally an idea whose benefits go far beyond campus boundaries.

On the other hand, recycling, too, has impacts on the environment. The production of recycled paper, for instance, requires removal of inks and clays, bleaching, water use, and energy consumption. Metals, glass, and plastics, when recycled, have their own impacts. The process of manufacturing with virgin materials carries a higher environmental price tag than is borne with recycling, but it is important to note that recycling is not totally benign.

Key Considerations in Developing Campus Recycling Programs

The goal of establishing an effective recycling program is challenging but achievable. The experiences of the many campuses that have succeeded illustrate a few key considerations.

Campus Waste Stream. It is important to know what materials show up in the campus waste stream, from which buildings, and at what point in the academic year. Most residential campuses produce 10 to 20 percent high-grade office paper, 10 percent newspaper, 20 to 30 percent corrugated cardboard containers, 10 to 20 percent leaves and yard waste, 15 to 25 percent food and dining service waste, and 10 percent used beverage containers, perhaps less in deposit law states. (These percentages exclude "special wastes" such as hazardous waste and construction and demolition debris.) While it is theoretically possible to recycle or compost virtually all of these wastes on most campuses, local markets or processing resources may preclude the recycling of more than half of the total waste stream. Most of the institutions profiled in Table 11.1 and Exhibit 11.1 began their recycling efforts with high-grade paper, a sizable fraction of the waste stream that is easily marketed in most areas of the country.

Each section of the campus, perhaps each building, yields a different waste profile depending on its function. The waste streams of academic and administrative buildings may contain up to 60 percent high-grade paper. Dining areas typically produce half food waste and half packaging (mostly corrugated cardboard boxes). Dormitories usually produce up to 30 percent newspaper, but little high-grade paper until semester's end when course syllabi and notes are discarded. For the past two years, students at the University of Wisconsin in Madison sponsored a special end-of-semester collection for notebooks and class notes in the Student Union. In spring 1991, two tons of this high-grade paper were recovered for recycling.

Seasonal trash tonnages can fluctuate dramatically. May and June are usually the heaviest months. For instance, the tonnage at Dartmouth College in December is consistently less than half of its June tonnage. At Brown University, in Providence, Rhode Island, up to 40 percent of annual trash tonnage (Spring, 1990) is generated at dormitory cleanout just prior to commencement, according to Harold Ward of the Center for Environmental Studies (see Corless and Ward, this volume). To reduce this cleanout waste at the University of Colorado, in Boulder, the student environmental group collects and stores furniture, carpeting, and other items for resale in September to entering students, resulting in handsome savings in disposal costs and good bargains for the students (see Table 11.1 and Exhibit 11.1).

Another seasonal recyclable commodity is leaves, which makes up the largest fraction of the autumn waste stream on many campuses. Composting on or near the campus offers a cheap disposal alternative and, within a few months, yields a soil amendment product much in demand by grounds maintenance departments in the growing season.

Existing Recycling Efforts. Another aspect of understanding the campus waste stream is knowledge of what recycling efforts are already in place. Many campuses learn that there is more recycling happening on campus than records indicate. At Harvard in 1990, the campus recycling program collected only thirty-two tons of white office paper. This was a surprisingly low figure, given that a Purchasing Department survey revealed that over one thousand tons of white office paper entered the campus annually. Most was not ending up in the landfill, however. Another survey showed that an estimated six hundred tons of paper was recycled by private wastepaper haulers in local salvage operations. In some buildings, paper is scavenged by custodians and computer operators for their own profit; in others, it is recycled by committed environmentalists maintaining decades-old volunteer programs. While it was disappointing to learn that revenues from the sale of this comparatively valuable material were not helping to support the recycling program, it was gratifying that the university was already recycling almost two-thirds of the white paper coming on campus. Surveys and audits of this kind can yield surprising information about existing recycling.

Used beverage containers are another item targeted by scavengers. In every state, the intrinsically high value of the metal makes aluminum cans the most highly prized commodity for recycling. In deposit law states, the designated bottles and cans carry redemption values that have students, janitors, and dumpster divers scurrying to pluck the materials from the waste stream.

Ongoing programs to reclaim, salvage, or compost materials also count in assessments of recycling tonnages. Many materials related to motor vehicle operations are recycled as a matter of course, such as motor oil, batteries, and scrap metals. Most campus food services collect and store cooking fats and oils for rendering, for example. A growing number of grounds maintenance departments mow grass clippings back into the turf, mulching the nutrients and avoiding substantial disposal costs.

Markets. A good understanding of local markets for recyclable commodities also is important. In the world of recycling, a "market" is a company that buys or accepts delivery of secondary materials for reprocessing. It may pay or charge for a given commodity. The fee is based on a formula that includes current commodity values, equipment costs, and hauling charges. Ideally, recycling costs the campus no more than trash disposal fees, although profitability is contingent on commodity value fluctuations. Awareness of market options and creative brokering have enabled some campuses to at least break even in recycling costs.

Markets are dynamic and local. Consider newspapers, a prominent fraction of the dormitory waste stream. Traditional markets for newsprint (boxboard manufacturers and recycling mills) may at times be glutted with postconsumer newsprint and lower grades of office paper. A market glut was reflected in the recycling processing fees of $30 to $50 per ton charged to many campus recycling programs late in 1991. Demand for newspaper is expected to increase steadily as large de-inking mills become operational throughout the 1990s. Legislation mandating that newspaper publishers use more recycled newsprint guarantees a market for recycled newsprint.

A new market for newspaper emerged for campuses located close to agricultural areas during the drought of 1988: animal bedding. Farmers in Vermont, Wisconsin, and elsewhere realized that shredded newspaper from the local university would provide cattle with bedding comparable to straw for considerably less than the $50 per ton cost (Morton, 1990). Newspaper used as bedding has proved safe for the animals, composts readily when mixed with manure, is convenient for the farmers, and has become a prime newspaper recycling option for some campuses.

A good source of market information with regional highlights is *Recycling Times,* a biweekly publication of the National Solid Wastes Management Association in Washington, D.C. *Resource Recycling,* a monthly published in Portland, Oregon, also reports on national market trends.

Labor Relations. If custodians are to be the chief agents in emptying bins and centralizing recyclables within buildings—which is the case in most institutionalized campus programs—issues related to custodial time and job definition must be addressed. Custodian support and involvement has proved crucial in building-by-building implementation of campus recycling programs, including factors such as bin type, size, and placement. Campus programs failing to elicit custodian input have faltered in their recycling programs and have missed the opportunity to build commitment among this important group of potential supporters.

Furthermore, custodians are typically the principal enforcers of the quality of the recyclable materials. Preferably by friendly policing of building occupants but ultimately by leaving rejected material behind, they are called on to ensure that the campus's recyclable commodities meet market specifications.

Custodians may have a personal reluctance to implement recycling if it means loss of income from scavenging. In bottle deposit law states, custodians may see revenues from container redemption as an unofficial but significant fringe benefit. Harvard allows local scavengers to keep whatever proceeds are generated by the program; other campuses, such as the University of Wisconsin in Madison, have banned custodians from keeping aluminum cans for personal profit.

Recycling adds to the workday and job responsibilities, and it requires a transitional period while custodians learn how to do the job. But after the initial kinks are worked out, most campuses find that recycling does not take a significant amount of time. Cornell University Buildings and Grounds found that recycling added only ten minutes per week to custodial work time. At many institutions, custodians compensate for the added duties by collecting office trash less often, sometimes only three nights per week, leaving the alternate nights for recyclables. Respect for custodians' needs for weight limits is also important. At Dartmouth College, custodian union rules state that workers can not pick up bundles or receptacles weighing more than twenty-five pounds (Skomra, 1989). This limit was an important factor in choosing recycling containers.

Safety. Concerns related to fire egress, combustibility, and sanitation are paramount on campuses. Fire codes preclude accumulation of recyclables in building hallways, stairways, and utility rooms. At Harvard, some older dormitories lack space for in-building storage of recyclables. Students were unsympathetic to objections to stacks of recyclables in every dormitory hallway until the municipal fire marshal cited the piles as violations of fire laws. In case of a panicked exit, he pointed out, students would have been unable to get down the stairs fast enough. Students are relatively content now to carry their recyclables to an adjacent building with more storage space.

Stacked piles of paper, glass, and metal are less combustible than comparable volumes of mixed trash. Absence of oxygen in paper piles will not sustain flames, although shredded paper and plastic bottles can be a serious fire hazard. The best protections against fire, as well as pest and vermin problems, are regular, reliable pickup service and secure storage. Some local fire regulations and campus building codes require sprinkler systems in recycling storage rooms. Many campus building codes also require that new building designs include adequate, secure space for recyclables.

Community Relations. Host communities may be affected by campus recycling programs. Campuses in or near communities that do not recycle may become vulnerable to loads of recyclables brought in from the outside that are put into campus recycling containers. This practice may not be unwelcome; Stanford and Denison have opened their recycling drop-off centers to the public as a community service (see Table 11.1 and Exhibit 11.1).

On the other hand, if the reverse is true, and there is curbside recycling offered to the residents of the surrounding city or town but not to members of the campus community, students or others may be tempted to set recyclables out for the town or city to recycle. Needless to say, in an era of $50 per ton charges for recycling newspaper, this practice can damage town-gown relations.

Coordination and Education. Recycling efficiency benefits from centralization. Haulers of recyclable materials and manufacturers of recycling containers offer discounts for large contracts. A campus that is well informed about how to prepare recyclables also produces more consistent results. Members of the campus community respond better to a program in which every building offers the same rules, container colors, and range of commodities recycled.

Coordination may require the cooperation of many branches of the campus: directors of grounds maintenance, custodial services, and food services, superintendents of laboratories, libraries, and classroom buildings, leaders of student environmental organizations, and environmentally minded faculty members. At large decentralized universities, where these individuals might number in the hundreds, direct coordination of all parties may be impossible, but campus recycling committees with representatives have been effective on campuses of all sizes. In any case, clear channels of communication must be established and maintained. Once started, the program must be monitored carefully and the campus population told of progress or setbacks. Newsletters sent to all parties have built and sustained commitment at many campuses.

Education and motivation are also important. Everyone needs to know why recycling is important, how to recycle, whom to call, and so on. Posters, pins, stickers, and other promotional techniques have all been used successfully. Contests can be beneficial; for example, Harvard's dormitories held an Ecolympics competition that measured per capita recycling rates as well as utility and water consumption and awarded the dormitory with the lowest environmental impact (see Keniry and Trelstad, this volume).

An understanding of attitudes and opinions is necessary in order to achieve high participation rates, though this is an area where little formal research has been done. Studies by Williams (1991) at the University of Massachusetts, in Amherst, and DeYoung (1986) at the University of Michigan point out that people will recycle if it is no more trouble than is disposal of trash. Most campuses try to consider the psychological dimension of recycling in planning. For example, it is important to place recycling and trash receptacles together. Recycling containers will accumulate a lot of trash unless trash bins are close by. Labeling, bin design, and other factors also influence participation. Even a logo helps: The University of Vermont's recycling containers all bear the campus catamount mascot as an instantly recognizable symbol for recycling.

Conclusion

Unlike the programs that started and disappeared in the 1970s, campus recycling is here to stay. Important as it is, however, recycling alone will not earn a campus a clean bill of environmental health. Waste reduction and reuse are far more effective ways of reducing environmental impact, and the goal should be a net reduction in the campus waste stream, not simply more recycling. Yet, recycling is among the most visible, measurable, and enforcable of the environmentally sound practices that a campus can undertake.

References

Baxter, C., and others. *Toward a System of Integrated Solid Waste Management: The Commonwealth Master Plan.* Boston: Commonwealth of Massachusetts, Department of Environmental Protection, 1990.

Ching, Raymond, and Coston, Vernie. "Mandatory Recycling at a Major University." In *Case Studies in Environmental Health and Safety.* Alexandria, Va.: Association of Physical Plant Administrators of Universities and Colleges, 1990.

DeYoung, Ray. "Encouraging Environmentally Appropriate Behavior: The Role of Intrinsic Motivation." *Journal of Environmental Systems,* 1986, *15,* 281-292.

Hargett, Teresa, and Osborn, Robert. "Cornell Recycles: A Major University Commitment." *Facilities Manager,* 1989, *5* (2), 40-47.

Janiak, Ann C. "Dartmouth Recycles Means Efficiently Managed Trash Disposal." *Executive Housekeeping Today,* 1990, *11* (7), 3, 4, 19.

Morton, Elaine. "Recycling Newspapers into Animal Bedding." *Association of Physical Plant Administrators of Universities and Colleges Newsletter,* 1990, *39* (6).

Skomra, Michelle. "Dartmouth Recycles: Is It The Solution to Waste Disposal Problems?" *Executive Housekeeping Today,* 1989, *10* (1), 5-6.

Spring, Scott. "The College's Recycling Efforts Right on Track." *Fortnightly: Dartmouth's Weekend Magazine,* February 9, 1990.

Student Environmental Action Coalition. *The Student Environmental Action Guide.* Berkeley, Calif.: EarthWorks Press, 1991.

Watson, Tom. "Recycling Goes to College." *Resource Recycling,* 1990, *10* (4), 76-81.

Williams, Elizabeth. "College Students and Recycling: Their Attitudes and Behaviors." *Journal of College Student Development,* 1991, *32* (1), 86-88.

RAYMOND CHING *is recycling coordinator for Rutgers, the State University of New Jersey. He is past president of the Association of New Jersey Recyclers and a former member of the National Recycling Coalition Board of Directors.*

ROBERT GOGAN *is recycling coordinator for the Harvard University Facilities Maintenance Department. He is a doctoral student in administration, planning, and social policy at the Harvard Graduate School of Education.*

INDEX

ORDERING INFORMATION

NEW DIRECTIONS FOR HIGHER EDUCATION is a series of paperback books that provides timely information and authoritative advice about major issues and administrative problems confronting every institution. Books in the series are published quarterly in Fall, Winter, Spring, and Summer and are available for purchase by subscription as well as by single copy.

SUBSCRIPTIONS for 1992 cost $45.00 for individuals (a savings of 20 percent over single-copy prices) and $60.00 for institutions, agencies, and libraries. Please do not send institutional checks for personal subscriptions. Standing orders are accepted.

SINGLE COPIES cost $14.95 when payment accompanies order. (California, New Jersey, New York, and Washington, D.C., residents please include appropriate sales tax.) Billed orders will be charged postage and handling.

DISCOUNTS FOR QUANTITY ORDERS are available. Please write to the address below for information.

ALL ORDERS must include either the name of an individual or an official purchase order number. Please submit your order as follows:
    Subscriptions: specify series and year subscription is to begin
    Single copies: include individual title code (such as HE1)

MAIL ALL ORDERS TO:
    Jossey-Bass Publishers
    350 Sansome Street
    San Francisco, California 94104

FOR SALES OUTSIDE OF THE UNITED STATES CONTACT:
    Maxwell Macmillan International Publishing Group
    866 Third Avenue
    New York, New York 10022

DATE DUE

"RESERVE"			
OCT - - 2000			
Display			
SEP 2 8 2004			
OCT 0 9 2006			
APR 1 5 2007 DEC 0 1 2007			

Demco, Inc. 38-293